Nation and Europe

Nation and Europe

In Lieu of Memoirs

JÁNOS MARTONYI

Helena History Press

Copyright 2023 © János Martonyi
All rights reserved

Published in the United States by:

H P

Helena History Press LLC
A division of KKL Publications LLC, Reno, NV USA
www.helenahistorypress.com
Publishing scholarship about and from Central and East Europe

This work was originally published as "Nemzet és Europa: Emlékirat helyett"
Martonyi János
Ludovika Egyetemi Kiadó
Budapest 2021
ISBN: 978-963-531-381-5

English edition: ISBN 978-1-943596-35-5

"Geographic Map of the V4 Countries" published with the kind permission of
Károly Kocsis & David Karácsonyi
CSFK Geographic Institute: Research Center for Astronomy and Earth Sciences.
Budapest, Hungary

Translator: Peter Pasztor
Copy editor: Jill Hannum and Krisztina Kós

Contents

Preface 1
Introduction 7

Part I. Tributes 41

International Law, European Law, Hungarian Law 43
Hungarian Foreign Policy, 896–1919 46
Reflections on Géza Herczegh's book 46
The Noble Banner of Human Rights 53
Acceptance Speech 57
In memoriam János Horváth 60
Otto von Habsburg: His Life and Legacy 63
Otto von Habsburg and Our Visions of Europe 68
A "Temporary Paradise" on the Road to Freedom 75
Speech Commemorating the Revolution and War of Independence
    in 1848–1849 78
Hungarian Diplomacy Day 82
Speech Commemorating Heroes' Day 85

Part II. World Trade in the Grip of Geopolitics 89

Investor-state Dispute Settlement and the Autonomy of EU Law:
    A Battle of Tribunals? 91
The New World Order 2018. Integration and Multipolarity 95
Geopolitics and World Trade 102
Book-launch Talk for *The Regional World Order: Transregionalism,
    Regional Integration, and Regional Projects across Europe and Asia.* 114

Part III. Still Europe… 121

The Visegrád Group, Central Europe, and the European Union 123
Different Perspectives – Common Interests 139
Presentation on the Role of Law and Identity in European Integration 147
Keynote Address to the Conference on the 70th anniversary of the
    foundation of the Council of Europe 156
The Schuman Declaration – Seventy Years Ago and Now 159
European Identity – To Open up or Close in 171

Times do change, and we change along with them, but we need to preserve more of what is constant—our history, our culture, our identity, and our values.

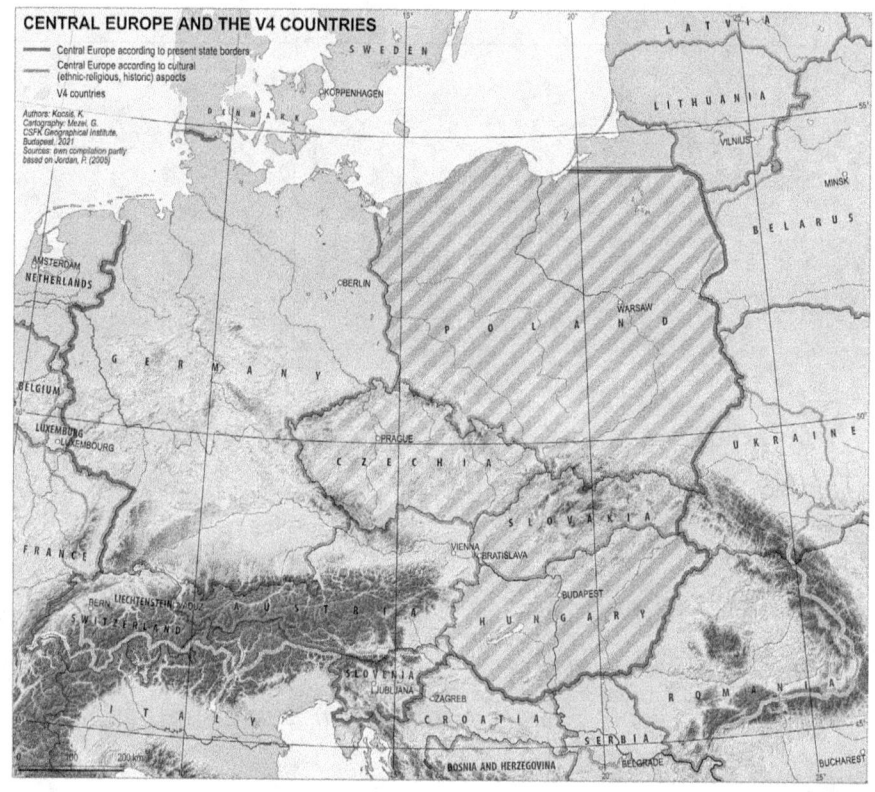

Preface

János Martonyi has been trying to scare us by saying that he will not write his memoirs and we should be satisfied with the volumes—almost a thousand pages—he has published. There is no doubt that the series that began with *Europe, Nation, Rule of Law* (1998) and now ends with *Nation and Europe* not only covers one of the most interesting periods in modern Hungarian social and political history but also offers readers an exciting intellectual journey. One might want to ask him: Does the fact that *Europe* is the first word in the title of the first volume but *nation* is the first one in the current title mean that the past twenty-plus years have rearranged his priorities? Tracing the career of the university professor, the lawyer, and the politician committed to public service, it can clearly be said that the nation has always been his first priority, but EU membership was undoubtedly the most prominent national strategic objective in the period of EU accession. These volumes plainly reveal the author's intellectual and political creed, his conservative-liberal patriotism, and his Euro-Atlantic commitment based on Hungarian national identity. As foreign minister, he consistently upheld the principles he formulated twenty-five years ago. "The essence of Europe lies in its diversity," he wrote. "If this diversity, with its many cultural and linguistic traditions, is laid waste or even dimmed, Europe will lose its identity. As a consequence, European unity cannot and will not exist without national identity, without the endurance and strengthening of the nation."[1]

---

[1] Martonyi, János: *Európa, nemzet, jogállam*. Budapest: Magyar Szemle—Európai Utas, 1998, 196.

Preface

The public health emergency caused by the Covid-19 virus and the ensuing economic crisis have for evermore highlighted the European Union's fragility and limited capacity to act. The 2015 migration crisis had already had serious civilizational and cultural consequences, challenging the European idea. During the pandemic crisis, as Martonyi himself writes, the response at the global-universal level failed spectacularly, and the EU institutions would have found it difficult to take decisions in the absence of health-policy competence. One lesson of the crisis is that it was too early to bury nation-states. Sovereign states provide the front line of defence in matters affecting people's livelihoods and basic security, and the role of borders and territory is undergoing reappraisal.

For all the turbulent changes taking place in the world, virtually all the writings of János Martonyi emphasize that "the essence of a conservative worldview is to seek and find elements of permanence, to preserve lasting values, even in the face of changes to the contrary. [...] The only way to preserve values is to recognize and accept the elements of permanence." He regards roots and the cultural dimension as important not only for the cultivation of national traditions but also in the construction of a European identity. Robert Schuman had considered European cultural heritage, indeed the very soul of Europe, as the foundation of European identity, and the author likewise also draws attention to the need to place the cultural-civilizational dimension, European identity, at the heart of European integration:

> We respect and accept the values of the Enlightenment, freedom, equality, and fraternity, without which Europe would never be what it is. But neither would Europe be Europe without its Judaeo-Christian heritage [...] Alongside the Acropolis and Golgotha, the Capitoline also played an important role because, without the legacy of Roman law, law could not have been both an indispensable means of establishing and running Community institutions, developing integration [...], and a central element of culture itself, European identity.[2]

However, he leaves no doubt that European integration must be built on the free federation of national cultural communities. And European integra-

---

2   Ibid., 197.

tion based on the cultural concept of nation, a supra-state Europe of nations, is in Hungary's national strategic interest. In several of his studies in this volume, Martonyi emphasizes that the sovereign Member States have relinquished their sovereignty neither in full nor in part, but have entrusted the exercise of part of their rights therefrom to the common EU institutions, i.e., they exercise these powers jointly. That is to say, state sovereignty is an indispensable legal basis for integration as a whole, which is not weakened but strengthened by the recognition of linguistic, cultural, and spiritual communities, just as the recognition of the existence of these communities would strengthen the European institutions.

One of the success stories of regional cooperation between sovereign states within the European Union is the invigoration of the Visegrád Group. From a geopolitical and security-policy point of view, the Central European region has also become greatly valued. The migration crisis strengthened the cohesion of the region, and the economic and various aspects of belonging together beyond economic and political interest have also emerged. The essay titled "The Visegrád Group, Central Europe, European Union" is not only a confession of love for Central Europe but also a set of very rational arguments stating that the future of the EU cannot be shaped without the intensive involvement of the V4. Central European identity is part of European identity, and the Visegrád cooperation is linked to the European Union by history, geography, and geopolitical and security interests.

For decades, János Martonyi has constantly insisted on his thesis that absolute sovereignty based on a homogeneous nation-state cannot be the solution for the community of all Hungarians, the Hungarian nation as a whole. He admits that in recent decades the vision of the defining role of the sovereign state representing the nation in European integration has indeed moved closer to Gaullism, but this has been driven by the spectacular strengthening of national identity in recent decades, not by the notion of the unlimited sovereignty of the homogeneous nation-state. Indeed, we are living in an era of the explosion of identity politics, with the radicalization of the Black Lives Matter movement on the left-liberal side giving new impetus to human-rights fundamentalism. And, on the conservative side, the idea of building the "circular defence" of national sovereignty around national identity and constitutional identity is gaining strength. With his conservative worldview, the former foreign minister is not awe-struck by the progressive identity war, probably believing that society outgrows such fads in time. The real challenge for European integration, he believes, is to recover the balance between economic integration, political union, and the cultural dimension. Identity, European culture, and the civilizational heritage must be rediscovered.

Now that the euphoria of accession is over, new Member States are increasingly determined to find their place in European integration and to make their national identities more visible. János Martonyi is not enthused by the widening gap between sovereignists and federalists, because he does not see the differences as being nearly as sharp as the political debates make them out to be. In his introductory essay, however, he details the problem of constitutional identity, defining where the boundary lies between the constitutional core of the legal order of the Member States and the primacy of European law, where the line of protection of the sovereignty of the Member States lies, beyond which the primacy of European law does not prevail. After the recent ruling of the *Bundesverfassungsgericht*, the question arises even more sharply whether the law of the European Union has an unconditional and absolute precedence over the law of the Member States, or whether this doctrine, developed by the European Court of Justice, can be limited by the Member States in certain cases through their constitutions or their constitutional courts.

Among these limits, the doctrine of *ultra vires*, i.e., the doctrine that EU institutions are not to exceed the limits of the powers conferred on them by the sovereign Member States, is of particular importance. The German Constitutional Court indirectly reprimanded the Court of Justice of the European Union (CJEU) in relation to the European Central Bank's (ECB) bond-buying programme, on the grounds that the ECB had breached the *ultra vires* prohibition and that the CJEU had failed to carry out the review necessary to establish the extension beyond powers. The ruling is an important milestone in defining the relationship between EU law and the laws of the Member States, making it clear that this relationship cannot be reduced to the primacy of EU law. Martonyi warns that the significance of the issue goes far beyond the dilemma of the conflict between the two sets of norms; it raises general theoretical and political questions about the future development of integration. What is needed is sensible restraint and mutual respect, which have room neither for creeping federalism by EU institutions nor excessive claims to sovereignty by some Member States.

Preface

Expounding a favourite theme, the relationship between geopolitics and world trade, Martonyi develops in eight theses his basic argument that geopolitical structure is not hierarchical but heterarchical. Although not hierarchical, a heterarchy is also an order, yet a variable one, a ranking established by different criteria (GDP, population, territory, defence capabilities, technology, etc.). And the sequence changing as per various criteria makes it clear that there is no single global hegemon. He senses the increasingly fierce struggle between China and the USA for dominance in the new world order, but he believes no binary world order reminiscent of the Cold War is likely to emerge, and the pandemic will not change that. Globalization will slacken, because the movement of data (digital explosion) rather than the movement of goods will be the focus, and supply chains will undergo a major transformation. In contrast to globalization, fragmentation, regionalization, and localization will become increasingly important as a conceptual framework, and the world will become more dangerous and less secure. I find it rather interesting that János Martonyi does not use the term "liberal world order" as a conceptual framework when describing global processes, and therefore he does not treat the erosion of the liberal world order and discusses these processes in a different conceptual framework.

In the *Tributes* part of this book, Martonyi includes his recollections of Géza Herczegh, Tom Lantos, József Antall, János Horváth, and Otto von Habsburg as though they were a continuation of the series entitled "People" in his 2015 volume. One might have the impression that, when he writes about Géza Herczegh, he is imagining himself in his subject's place, launching his unwritten memoir. A man driven by values, a realist driven by values, Herczegh saw the essence of the world in its cultural nature. The deepest, strongest layer of his personality was his Hungarian identity. He was profoundly wise and unbiassed, critical yet inoffensive, calmly serene. The great dilemma of his life was whether to be a realist or to uphold fundamental values, even at the cost of heavy sacrifices.

János Martonyi has held on to his civic mindedness, just as his father had tried to insist on his own civic way of life, never giving up his liberalism, his commitment to Christian democracy, and the national cause.

János Martonyi and I became friends, we clocked up four difficult years in office in a pro-civic government between 1998 and 2002, and together we

Preface

campaigned to reverse the tide in the second election round. Since then, we have met regularly, and fought tennis matches and played cards to the death.

I heartily recommend this volume to anyone seeking answers to the challenges of national politics and global world order today.

Budapest, 30 September 2020.
István Stumpf
University Professor, former Chancellery Minister,
former Constitutional Court Judge

Introduction

This volume is a continuation—indeed a reiteration—of messages contained in three previous volumes. *Europe, Nation, Rule of Law*[1] was published twenty-two yearss ago, in 1998; *We and the World*,[2] which contains my writings from 2002 to 2010, was published in 2015; and *Openness and Identity: Geopolitics, World Trade, Europe*[3] appeared in 2018. The titles encapsulate in brief the books' otherwise generically and thematically varied content and the main ideas defining it. These ideas have evolved and adapted to changing circumstances over the decades, but their essence has remained unchanged. This is why the collection of writings and talks of these last three years can be seen not simply as a continuation, a tracking of change, but as a persistent attempt to reiterate elements of permanence. For all the changes the world undergoes, its essence, people, their most important communities, above all the nation, the sense and experience of national belonging, the history, values, moral norms of humanity, and their origins do not change. Human nature is more perceptive of change and more attentive to the processes that bring about alteration. Elements of continuity and permanence tend to receive less attention, while change attracts more attention, prompts reflection, the drawing of conclusions, the making of proposals for even larger-scale changes, or—perhaps engendering trouble—the advancement of all-encompassing theories and ideologies. Research has shown that, for various reasons,

---

1   Martonyi, János : *Európa, nemzet, jogállam*. Budapest, Magyar Szemle – Európai Utas, 1998.
2   Martonyi, János: *Mi és a világ*. Budapest, Magyar Szemle Alapítvány, 2015.
3   Martonyi, János: *Nyitás és identitás. Geopolitika, világkereskedelem, Európa*. Szeged, Pólay Elemér Alapítvány, 2018.

Introduction

we perceive change as overwhelmingly negative, despite the fact that the world has, on the whole, fared better, not worse, in terms of the most important indicators not only over the last two thousand years but even in the last seventy years, however difficult it may be to say so as I write the in the midst of the Covid pandemic with its unforeseeable and grave consequences.

In this volume, the essay written on the occasion of the 70th anniversary of the Schuman Declaration wishes to underline that the essence of a conservative worldview is to seek and find elements of permanence, to preserve lasting values even in the face of changes to the contrary. While a progressive approach would want to accelerate changes "required by historical necessity," a conservative one would attempt to slow them down at least. Change per se is therefore not a good or positive phenomenon, even if it is inevitable. The only way to preserve values is to recognize and accept the elements of permanence.

The immanent essence of Europe, the nation, and the rule of law has not changed, only the circumstances, the conditions, the requirements, the challenges have altered and created new needs for adaptation. Our place in the world is constantly evolving and is of course the subject of external and internal debate. Enormous and profound changes are taking place in the world's economy and trade, its security, and geopolitical structure; yet, from the Hungarian point of view, nothing has changed, and nothing will change. "No matter what happens," we have been here for a thousand years, and we will remain here, both as individuals and as a national community, preserving our Hungarian identity, our European identity, and the true values and requirements of the rule of law. In other words, we maintain and strengthen our individual and communal, and therefore our national, identity by being open to the world, by knowing and preserving where we belong.[4]

And the world remains—increasingly—exposed to global challenges, the scope, severity, and threat of which are variable and contested, as are the causes and ways of addressing them, including effective action and the level and content of regulation within it. It is difficult to dispute that universal (global), continental (European), state and even sub-state, and local action is needed in terms of both regulation and concrete measures, the big issue however is at which level these rules and measures are most reasonable, effective, and

---

[4] Nagy, Csongor István: "Martonyi János: *Nyitás és identitás – Geopolitika, világkereskedelem, Európa*". *Magyar Jog,* volume 66 (2019), number 1, 63–64.

Introduction

democratic, i.e., where the democratic legitimacy behind them is strongest. The latter is also a fundamental condition of effectiveness and success. Finding the right balance between the different levels of regulation and decision-making is one of the most important and controversial issues of our time. Underlying this, of course, are fundamental geopolitical, economic, and power concerns and interests. It is no coincidence that at both the global and European level the question of division of competences and the relationship between of these levels has become one of the most important political—and therefore power—issues in recent years and has consequently become a major focus of interest in international law, European law, and the constitutional laws of the Member States. Ultimately, the relationship between the norms of international, European, and constitutional law, the relevant case law, and the related theoretical and political debates reflect the evolution and changes in the geopolitical structure of the world, which has been shifting from hierarchy to heterarchy for decades. The relationship between the levels of decision-making is therefore evolving in line with the changing geopolitical structure and economic power relations, and the world is constantly being transformed in this respect too, while competition between the levels of decision-making has variable outcomes but is a constant element.

Times do change, and we change along with them, but we need to preserve more of what is constant—our history, our culture, our identity, and our values. It is a serious problem if we lag behind the changes, if we fail to perceive the need to alter our thought, attitudes, policies, and institutions in the way these changes demand, but it is at least as bad if we only perceive and overestimate the need to change and fashion all-embracing theories and ideologies to radically transform, subvert, and "renew" the world.

One of the characteristics of major changes is that they are difficult or impossible to foresee. That does not prevent us from constantly predicting the future, providing accurate forecasts about the way things will develop. Economically, in domestic and foreign policy, and, especially in economics, we express this in figures. We increasingly live within a framework of "forecasting," while reality often turns out to be quite different from what the forecasts suggested. Unexpected events occur, triggering new sequences of events, giving new directions to processes begun earlier, or even accelerating or slowing them down. Nevertheless, foresight is essential, because without it no

Introduction

human society, community, state, or institution can function. Some twenty-five years ago, I myself made the following vague predictions:

> The disconnection of the world of finance from real production and economic processes, the ever widening gap between wealth and poverty, growing work shortages and the extreme disproportionalities of distribution, the lack of transparency, insecurity, and abuse resulting from the concentration of power and domination structures, and the ostensibly unstoppable increase in environmental damage not only represent a real and objective threat in themselves but can also provoke false and dangerous subjective reactions on the part of the intelligentsia, as had happened in earlier periods. Just as the glaring social injustices of the nineteenth century engendered the mass-murdering fundamentalism of the twentieth century that we now call Marxism-Leninism. Just as the genuine injustices of the peace system that concluded the First World War contributed to the rise of Nazism. In the same way, the growing contradictions at the end of the twentieth century can give rise to new fundamentalist and totalitarian ideologies. In the wake of these fundamentalist ideologies, new vanguards may come to the fore claiming to be the sole possessors of the "scientific" theory and practice of addressing threats, and demand total and exclusive power to avert dangers and solve problems. Thus, once again, a legitimate and justified need to solve problems can become a greater disaster than the ones we were trying to avert.[5]

The 2008 financial crisis and the ensuing economic- and sovereign-debt crises are over (although the causes have not yet been satisfactorily eliminated), and today the world is facing a new, much more serious and complex crisis—indeed, several crises. Less comprehensive and unified than before, the new (old?) fundamentalist ideologies are lurking among us and are even triggering increasingly powerful social and political explosions. Colours are not always precisely identifiable; red, green, and brown are mixed, but the symptoms are similar regardless of colour and are difficult to separate, especially

---

[5] Martonyi, János: „Miért, hogyan, hol és mit rontottunk el?" In idem: *Európa, nemzet, jogállam*. Budapest, Magyar Szemle – Európai Utas, 1998, 136; also in Fasang, Árpád (ed.): *Az (magyar) értelmiség hivatása*. Budapest, Mundus, 1997.

Introduction

when one colour—red, for example—is painted on top of another. Extreme simplifications in worldview and anger lead straight to violence. It does not help either when many respond to this with the intellectual superiority of omniscience and the moral superiority of a monopoly on truth.

The global threats to humankind are becoming increasingly acute and are of growing concern to more and more people. Views differ on the causes, the severity of the dangers, how to tackle them, the level and means of action, but there are fairly clear indications that the dangers are likely to materialize. The fragility of the global financial system and its consequences were illustrated by the 2008 financial- and sovereign-debt crisis, and the debate over the effectiveness of international, European, and state action has not abated ever since. It is widely accepted that, while the international trading system has basically performed well, not falling into the trap of protectionism, the various—multilateral, regional, and state level—trade-policy responses have generally been satisfactory and have helped to overcome the crisis, the monetary policies were slow to respond, and fiscal policies, notably in the case of the European Union, exacerbated the situation rather than alleviate it in some respects. In any event, the warning of the possibility of a more serious crisis has been delivered, and the question remains whether this warning was forceful enough at global or European level to enable us to tackle the consequences of the ensuing crisis in all areas and at all levels.

In 2015, the world, and Europe in particular, received a stark warning of the onset of global migration. The phenomenon itself is, of course, is as old as humanity and has been present throughout history. It may have been triggered by changes in climate and the natural environment in general, famines, water and food shortages, natural disasters, overpopulation, epidemics, and, of course, people themselves, with their wars, genocides, massacres, power struggles, and all that this leads to.

In most cases, global risks cause and reinforce each other. This was the case with the 2015 migration crisis, when drought caused food shortages, and famine (and of course brutal dictatorships) triggered mass movements; the response led to civil war, and war set off mass migration towards Europe. There have been similar events before, but the 2015 crisis highlighted with unprecedented force both the interrelation of global risks and the reality of the regional and local impact of these risks. The crisis had serious economic, social, political, civilizational, and cultural consequences, including a particular challenge for Europe and the European way of life. Member States responded to this challenge with divergent policies, reflecting the significant differences between their historical, geographical, economic, and cultural heritages, and these responses were exacerbated by ideological and cultural tensions among political camps. The local impact of the global risk thus led to a series of security, ideological, moral, economic, demographic, and cultural dilemmas, themselves conflicting with each other, and thus did not facilitate the prevention of the threat.

The current pandemic is an example of recurring disasters that have threatened humanity for thousands of years. Epidemics have always existed, and pandemics as global risks have been treated to all the relevant analyses. In recent decades, clear predictions of the emergence of various forms of coronavirus have been put forward, and warnings, not just concerns, about the safety of scientific experiments on viruses have also been formulated. Covid-19's origins and causes will be debated for many years to come, and the dispute is unlikely to ever be definitively and unequivocally settled.

The Covid-19 pandemic is accompanied by an *infodemic,* the appearance of masses of analyses, studies, treatises, essays, and it would be an impossible undertaking to even provide a bibliography of a fraction of the writings already published. The impact of the pandemic is inestimable and will affect every aspect of society––the economy, science, technology, culture, human- and community life. Many have said that the world will never be the same as it was before the pandemic, and, though this is true, the world keeps changing regardless of the great crises and shocks, only it does so more slowly and less spectacularly.

The essence of the world and of human existence, however, remains constant and unchanging. Crises often accelerate or slow down processes that have already begun or give them a new direction. The study entitled "Geopolitics and World Trade" included in this volume attempts to summarize the essence of the geopolitical and world economic structure and processes in 2018 in eight theses. It is perhaps worth considering these eight theses in the light of the pandemic; whether, and to what extent, they are valid in the world situation it has brought about. The attempt is useful in spite of the fact that the one thing there is currently general agreement on is that the outcome, impact, and consequences of the pandemic cannot be assessed in any single area, and that no estimate is likely to hold water. What makes anticipation even more difficult is that unpredictable consequences in differ-

Introduction

ent areas interact with each other, and thus it would be an equation with infinite unknowns.

The validity of each of the eight theses is affected by certain general factors, all of which have been amplified by the pandemic. In any major crisis, the role, importance, and responsibility of the exercise of public power, of government, increases. The scope for decision-making becomes wider and weightier, and the differences between the impact of good and bad public policies multiply. Bad decisions can have unforeseeable consequences, and the impact of small mistakes and omissions can be enormous. This is particularly true of political consequences, since it is in times of crisis that the quality of government becomes really important in the eyes of the governed, and it is in times of crisis that the public is primarily capable of judging whether or not it can trust those that exercise public power, and whether or not it can get from them the good and right decisions that it expected when entrusting them with the task and responsibility of governing. The stakes for public power are thus raised enormously, with good government "sweeping the board" and bad government "being worsted."

This increase in the role and responsibility of public power amplifies the importance of the decision-making and regulatory levels and brings to the fore the issues of interrelations—including tensions and conflicts—among them. It is no coincidence that the clashes between the decision-making levels of global, regional (European), and sovereign states, and the division of competences and responsibilities among universal international organizations, the European Union, and its Member States, take on a particular significance in times of crisis and become the subject of heated political and legal debate. One natural element of these debates is the question of the responsibility for the outbreak and management of the crisis and its distribution between the different levels. This is particularly the case in the situation where the global-universal level failed spectacularly, and doubts arose with regard to the European level, as well. Of course, it must be taken into account that multilateral international organizations and integration institutions exercise only as much authority as the contracting parties or Member States entrust them with. In the absence of health powers, for example, it would have been difficult for the EU institutions to take independent decisions, and it is the Member States that are to be held to account for the lack of solidarity. As a materialized global risk, however, the pandemic raised with unprecedented clarity the dilemmas of the relationship between the regulatory and the decision-making levels. The lessons learned will give new impetus to the theoretical, political, and competence debates on this issue. What can already be concluded is that, in vital and existential matters that affect people's lives, survival, and basic security, public authority, especially the sovereign state, with its territory and borders is indispensable, since it provides the means of defence, territorial protection. However, regional and local sub-state factors also come to the fore, as has been the case in major epidemics throughout history (during plagues, travellers were held up at city gates). It is noteworthy that in some European countries restrictive measures had to be imposed at the regional level, and regional identities strengthened in this context, perhaps also because of the dissatisfaction with the central government (for example, in the wake of the pandemic the proportion of supporters of Scottish independence rose by 5 percent, from 49 percent to 54 percent.)

But the role and responsibility of public power, government, in economic policy decisions is also of paramount importance in crises. As noted, international trade policy responded well to the 2008 crisis, and the multilateral trading system stood the test. Monetary and fiscal policies in particular fared much less well, the latter's mistakes largely causing the sovereign debt crisis. In the context of the current pandemic, the situation and consequences are more grave and more unpredictable. Yet, after the initial uncertainties there seems to be greater concord among trade, monetary, and fiscal policies. Nevertheless, given the progress of the health situation the economic and social consequences cannot be anticipated.

It is an open question to what extent the increased roles and responsibilities of different levels of public power as a result of the crisis will be lasting, especially given the rise and growing power of the technology giants. In the longer term, it will have to be decided whether some form of directly or at least indirectly legitimized public power or *big data* will govern the world. Another way to put the question is whether public power at various international, European, and national levels is capable of regulating and controlling, or even taxing the technology giants, or whether the latter are going to take over important decision-making levels of public power (as we have seen in certain cases). This latter phenomenon is also noteworthy because it anticipates the imaginary situation where human-made machines gradually come to rule humans. In any event, crises may help us to realize that public power

Introduction

cannot cede the burden and responsibility of government to anyone, let alone Google, Amazon or even Alibaba ... (though the Chinese trend seems to point in the opposite direction, that is, toward increasing state power).

In addition to and in relation to the growing role of public power, or government, two other interrelated issues increase in importance in any major crisis. One is territory, and the other is security. As a result of scientific and technological developments, state territory has become less and less significant in the world's power and geopolitical structures. However, a more forceful emergence of some global threats, the risks to energy, water, and food supplies, have led to a renewed recognition that territory is not only a fundamental condition of the survival and security of human communities but is also an indispensable factor in the existence of sovereign states, the exercise of public power. Territory is also an essential—though by no means the only—element in the world's geopolitical and economic structure. The 2015 crisis of migration in Europe likewise highlighted the significance of the role of territory, making the many-thousand-year-old thesis abundantly clear again that there can be no state without territory; that, by its very essence, its territory must be legally and physically delimited; and that it must have the capacity to defend its borders when necessary.

However, the issue of security in the context of public power and territory does not only arise in a time of crisis. Security itself has become an incomparably broader and more diverse category than ever before. Physical security with appropriate defence is only one among the many dimensions of security policy and is perhaps not the most important one. Advances in technology have brought up the issue of cybersecurity, the dangers of which are equal to the global threat that has been posed by thermonuclear weapons for decades. However, energy security, food security, and economic security in general have likewise become realities. It has also become clear that security is one and indivisible, in terms of both geography and area, and that threats to one area immediately spread to others, so that security policy must embrace every arena and address them as a whole. This has been the case for quite some while. Security policy having formerly focused only on the context of biological and chemical weapons, Covid-19 has made the issue of biosecurity glaringly obvious and tangible (though the global threat of epidemics had been the subject of some attention, especially in recent decades). Addressing this security risk will require much more attention and further material and intellectual resources at all levels of regulation and decision-making in the future. Currently, the world is devoting the majority of these resources to the development of and defense against military capabilities, nuclear weapons in particular. These weapons cannot be deployed against viruses, global warming or illegal migration, and the resources wasted on them are largely lost.

Security threats are therefore expanding into newer and newer areas, and the process of their expansion is inexorable and unpredictable. New and unknown risks arise, for which it is almost impossible to prepare—for, as we all know, war offices are always preparing for the last war.

There is now broad consensus on the general theses that the pandemic amplified the role and responsibility of public authority and the importance of territory and security. However, there is no such consensus on its geopolitical, economic, and commercial consequences. Some say that globalization is coming to an end, others say that a new era of genuine global cooperation is dawning. Many predict or even welcome the advent of a new world order led by China, while others believe that the pandemic will precipitate crisis in a Chinese economic and political system beset by latent internal problems and the decline of the empire. Whatever the outcome, answers to the questions at issue will, again, be largely provided by the unfolding of processes already begun, whether they will accelerate, slow down or take a new direction.

Also included in this volume is my 2019 paper on the relationship between geopolitics and world trade, which proposed eight theses for discussion. The first two argued that the geopolitical structure is characterized not by hierarchy but by heterarchy. Not hierarchical, a heterarchy is also an order yet a changing one, a ranking established by different criteria. Thus, the rankings differ by area—GDP, population, territory, defence capabilities, technology, etc.[6] And the variable rankings based on different criteria make it clear that there is no single global hegemon. Attempts have often been made to achieve this, but in recorded history no one has ever succeeded. But after the pandemic, the question arises: will this be the case in the future? The probability is that it will. There will no longer be a single global hegemon, or even if there should be, a world order based on hegemony would not last long.

---

6   On rankings data, see Szapáry, György and János Plósz Dániel, "Geopolitikai irányváltások a kialakulóban lévő új világrendben." *Hitelintézeti Szemle*, 18 (2019), 4, 112–129. http://doi.org/10.25201/HSZ.18.4.112129

Introduction

From the perspective at the time of this writing in August 2020, whether China or the United States will benefit from the pandemic in the increasingly fierce competition between the two superpowers is a question that most analysts now weigh in favour of China, and the dramatic differences in the medical management of the pandemic, the scale of the economic downturn, and, above all, the severity of the social and political consequences, suggest that this is indeed the case so far. It should also be remembered that China had taken the lead in the competition before the pandemic, not only because of the pace of its economic growth but also because of its spectacular technological advances. The pandemic therefore accelerates the process already begun to China's advantage. However, it is impossible to predict today how China's internal processes, especially on the periphery of the empire, will evolve, whether a social and political crisis will unfurl exploding the political system under dramatically increasing tight control or possibly lead to a Soviet-style stagnation. Those foreseeing the advance of the US overwhelmingly refer to the growing internal dangers and fragility of the Chinese political and social system.

There is, however, a third view, which, for different reasons, predicts that both superpowers will be weakened and lose ground as a consequence of the pandemic. This in turn could lead to the economic and geopolitical strengthening of other actors, the de facto rise of a multi-actor world order, the accentuation of heterarchy, and a turn towards disorder and anarchy. Will the pandemic thus ultimately be a portent and precursor of much-discussed chaos? This is as unlikely as the rise and perpetuation of a hierarchical world order based on a single hegemon. However the relationship between the two strongest powers develops, there will always be a third, a fourth or a fifth actor, and there will always be emerging powers forming alliances to break the unilateral hegemony. The essence of the structure will therefore remain, but power relations will change, most probably in favour of China. There will be no single centre of power, either at the state or non-state level.

The third thesis proposed that a binary world order reminiscent of the Cold War, i.e., two opposing economic and political systems, would not come into being because not only the geopolitical but also, more importantly, the ideological conditions for this were lacking. The pandemic has therefore not changed this third thesis.

The fourth thesis claimed that the two fundamental factors determining the development of the world order, security policy and trade policy, would

Introduction

converge, and that the instruments of these policies would partially fuse. Given that one of the major consequences of the pandemic was the rise to prominence of all the diverse dimensions of security, it is not surprising that security-policy considerations and instruments have come to play an increasingly important role in economic and commercial policy. Regulations to control and restrict foreign investment have been and continue to be adopted at various decision-making levels for security reasons. The national security exception under Article XXI of the GATT has come to be widely invoked, and there is an increasing number of disputes on whether restrictive measures based on national security interests can be subject to legal review and dispute settlement. Though the debate is essentially irresolvable, the rulings adopted under the WTO dispute settlement procedure do not support the US position that this reference in itself and by definition precludes the initiation of any dispute.[7]

Apart from questions of geopolitical and economic world order and power structure, it was on the future of the set of "symptoms" called globalization (as diversely defined) that the pandemic generated the most debate. Will the pandemic really put an end to globalization, will the process be transformed and acquire new forms, or will it be business as usual after the shock and setback abate? The sixth thesis stated that economic globalization would slow down. One sign of this is that a trend of many decades reversed a few years ago, and that global trade is no longer the engine of growth in the world economy, with trade in goods actually growing more slowly than global GDP. Apart from geopolitical and security factors, the reason for the slowdown in globalization is technological advance, which makes the transfer of data, rather than the movement of goods, possible and beneficial.

There is no doubt that the pandemic has augmented this slowdown, and the trend is likely to continue in the future. But globalization is not going to end even in the world economy and world trade. However, it is also possible that the process will return to its old course and continue unabated. The decline in world trade, which has so far outstripped the decline in the economy,

---

7   See Nagy, Csongor István, "Clash of trade and national public interest in WTO law: the illusion of 'weighing and balancing' and the theory of reservation," *Journal of International Economic Law*, volume 23, number 1, March 2020, 143–163. https://doi.org/10.1093/jiel/jgz028; see also idem: "A reconceptualization of WTO law's security exceptions: squaring the circle and judicializing national security," *Currents: Journal of International Economic Law*, volume 24, number 2, 2021, 49–59, 2.

will end in the absence of further shocks, and international trade in goods and services will begin to grow, but the pandemic has elicited significant and lasting changes. Primarily, supply chains are undergoing a major transformation as a result of three interrelated factors. First, production and activities previously offshored are "reshored," which of course has its reasonable limits, but health and safety considerations are going to overrule an economic rationale in the production of certain irreplaceable goods, particularly if technological progress further reduces the benefits of offshoring. Second, supply sources are diversified, reducing one-sided dependencies, as the shortages in the wake of the pandemic have highlighted the resulting security risks. Third, instead of on-time deliveries, formerly forgotten and neglected stockpiling has increased. Overall, the triad of reshoring, diversifying, and stockpiling significantly reduces the global and even regional system of supply- and value chains. This is intensified by the tendency to foreshorten these chains for security, sustainability, and economic considerations, particularly in relation to trade in agricultural products.

In the realms of economy and commerce, all this has accelerated a process that had begun earlier, engendering fragmentation, regionalization, and localization as opposed to globalization. It has also restrained the most important factor in globalization, foreign direct investment, since, as noted, the pandemic and the ensuing and aggravating tensions have made the security considerations that had already been taken into account even weightier.

However, this only applies to the economic dimension of globalization. In the wake of a shock, science and technology develop in leaps and bounds, as they have after wars for instance. We are already witnessing a digital explosion caused by the necessities of the pandemic. New means of global connectivity have emerged, transforming and redefining the role of geographical distance in connecting people. The volume of trade in goods and international capital flows may be reduced, but data flows are growing unstoppably, despite efforts to control them. However, not everything can be digitized; in keeping with their biological and social essence, people want to and will continue to meet each other.

It is bad news that the pandemic has raised the stakes of economic and geopolitical competition, deepened the gap between winners and losers, affected diverse countries, groups, and individuals differently and unequally. It has increased inequality, heightened geopolitical, economic, and trade con-

Introduction

flicts and the tensions that arise partly from these conflicts and partly from individual and especially collective neuroses. All in all, the world has become a more dangerous and a less secure place. This was the eighth thesis, which argued that the dangers threatening the world were worsening and the global risks caused by humanity were increasing. However, fundamental values and norms and the human will they represent, coupled with faith and knowledge, will be able to cope with threats known and unknown at the time.

This holds for the pandemic caused by Covid-19 and its unforeseeable consequences. Insofar as public authority fulfils its responsibilities at all levels; the various levels of decision-making and regulation focus on their own responsibilities rather than on entering jurisdictional dispute and conflict. The primary authority and responsibility of the sovereign state in matters affecting the security of its people, including the protection of the borders of communities organized into states, should unconditionally prevail; and states should focus on cooperation rather than on tensions among themselves and shifting the blame onto each other.

Covid-19 has thus really changed the world. Just like previous pandemics and other major shocks that have claimed many more victims than the current one. The same will happen in the event of future global hazards or other as yet unforeseen shocks. However, the major social, economic, cultural, technological, and demographic changes that they trigger will always have elements of permanence, even though we naturally pay much less attention to them as the world is driven by change. Not necessarily always in the right direction. This also applies to the major changes in factors defining world order, global geopolitics, world trade, the balance of power, and the resulting structural transformations. Yet, the shock has largely reinforced processes that had already been underway even in these areas, exposing existing weaknesses and mobilizing existing resources. What the ratio of continuity to change will be, we will only be able to assess in retrospect, and we will obviously not agree on it either.

As I have indicated, this volume is a continuation of the work published over the past twenty-five years and is in no small part a reiteration of the messages contained in them. This naturally applies to all the reflections I have set down in writing on the concept of nation, national identity, Europe, European integration, its successes, dilemmas, crises, and future. This holds true especially to the relationship between national and European identity, the

Introduction

unqualified primacy of the former, to the compatibility of the two identities, to the concepts of the nation and the sovereign state, and to their differences and relationship, to the possible ways of resolving their dilemmas, and, ultimately, to the linking of Hungarian national and Hungarian Europe policies, their implementations mutually reinforcing each other. It applies to the issues that have been—in this order—the most important for me, with a slight exaggeration, in three times twenty-five years.

This does not mean that the world, the changing circumstances, the changing conditions, and the new challenges have not influenced my views. What has not changed, however, is the bottom line. This is what I formulated twenty-five years ago:

> The essence of the European integration process lies in upholding and even strengthening national identity. The essence of Europe lies in its diversity. If this diversity, with its many cultural and linguistic traditions, is laid to waste or even dimmed, Europe will lose its identity. As a consequence, European unity cannot and will not exist without national identity, without the endurance and strengthening of the nation.
> It is therefore more accurate to talk about supra-state Europe than supranational Europe. The integration process weakens the nation-state, weakens the omnipotent state, which, in the worst case, considers itself a homogeneous nation-state even if it is not one. It will shrink back from anything in order to achieve homogeneity. Among other things, it ignores the nation as a category, refusing to acknowledge that the concepts of nation and state do not coincide in many parts of the world, not only in East-Central Europe.
> When we think about a stronger, a federal Europe, the aim is not to weaken the nation but quite the opposite. A truly united Europe can only be created if each nation pools its cultural, historical, and linguistic heritage to enrich and fulfil European integration.[8]

---

8   Martonyi, János, "A magyar nemzet sorsa és az európai fejlődés", in idem, *Európa, nemzet, jogállam*. Budapest, Magyar Szemle – Európai Utas, 1998, 125–132; also in: Kurucz, Gyula (ed.), *Nemzetstratégia a harmadik évezred küszöbén. A Magyarok IV. Világkongresszusának Nemzetstratégiai tanácskozásán (1996. jún. 15–16.) elhangzott előadások.* 1996.

Introduction

As for the changes, László Trócsányi gave a brilliant summary of them in his essay "Monnet, de Gaulle, and Post-global Challenges in János Martonyi's Worldview,"[9] in which he reviewed my 2018 book, *Openness and Identity*. I was so taken by the argument and momentum of the essay that I forgot to argue with it. There is no doubt that the developments of the past decades have brought me closer to de Gaulle's vision of the world, his foreign policy, and his vision of Europe in general. Brexit was only the last stage in the process, not even the most important one, of which the General had an inkling a good half a century earlier. It was no coincidence that British accession could only take place after his resignation and his death shortly afterwards. (As a matter of fact, he had been wrong to prevent British accession. Without the British—the English, in the eyes of the General—European integration would not never have reached the stage it did after many crises, challenges, and debates up to the point of Brexit. It is another matter that the British had never felt at home in the Community, not to mention in the Union.) In that the sovereign state representing the nation has a dominant role in European integration, I did indeed come close to a Gaullist vision, but this was based on the spectacular strengthening of national identity in recent decades, not on a notion of the unlimited sovereignty of a homogeneous nation-state. Not as fortunate as France, our nation is forced to live in several states; for us, the concepts of nation and state are not identical, the borders of the two do not coincide, and absolute sovereignty based on a homogeneous nation-state cannot be the solution for the Hungarian nation as a whole.

When the French and then the Dutch blocked the Constitutional Treaty in a referendum fifteen years ago, on 29 May 2005, this is what I penned:

> It was 30 August 1954. After a protracted debate, the French National Assembly *sine die* adjourned the ratification of the treaty on the European Defence Community, thereby finally killing the treaty France had initiated in May 1952 and effectively applied as of September 1952. The same happened with the Statute for a European Political Community, which provided, among other things, for a common foreign policy and a Community market. The event caused general consternation, as the idea had

---

9   Trócsányi, László, "Monnet, de Gaulle és a poszt-globális kihívások Martonyi János világképében". *Magyar Szemle*, volume 28 (2018), number 9–10, 13–23.

Introduction

originated in French foreign-policy circles, and its primary aim was to include (West) Germany in the Western alliance system and the process of European integration. The decision of the National Assembly was based on an odd combination, an ad hoc alliance between the then very strong French Communists and the Gaullists. Both political forces, for radically different reasons, decided not to support the creation of European political union. The French Communist Party followed the instructions of the Soviet Union, which had been putting enormous pressure on the French to drop the treaty, and the Gaullists demonstrated their independence in the face of the United States, which also pressurized them to ratify the treaty. [...]

All this is now history. Or is it not? Before crying over the parallels between 30 August 1954 and 29 May 2005, it is worth recalling that just a few months after the decision of the National Assembly and the general shock in Europe, the Benelux Memorandum was drafted, setting in motion an unstoppable process of economic integration, which has gradually and steadily strengthened, expanded, and has essentially been successful. The advocates of a united Europe did not give up but understood that in the prevalent historical situation something fundamentally different was needed, that politics and public opinion had different preferences, and that it was therefore necessary to rethink matters and build on the already existing, successful elements (the Coal and Steel Community) to lay the foundations from which the original dream of European unity could later be realized. [...]

European unity means something quite different today than it did half a century ago. Success not only attracts but can also repel and arouse mistrust. The linguistic redefinition of reality is dangerous even in the terms of European integration (perhaps that which is not a constitution, especially in the strict legal sense, should never have been called a constitution), and the professional and moral strength of European institutions, which had initially enjoyed great prestige, should never have been allowed to be largely used for the exercise and subtle, barely perceptible abuse of power. (Nor would it have been a disadvantage if the citizens of Western Europe had been informed of the essence of enlargement, i.e., reunification in good time, for it is easier to frighten and deceive the average citizen who can name but two or three of the accession countries at best.)

Introduction

The result of all this and much more is an identity crisis that extends far beyond the borders of France and cannot be explained by the internal political situation, the economic and social circumstances of a single Member State. Coincidence is never coincidence in the true sense of the word, and the irrational can be rationally explained. Europe has now been given an opportunity to examine itself, its successes and failures, and to learn from the crisis, because it had experienced crises before and had always been able to overcome them.

The consequences should not be belittled of course, because they are grave also in terms of the development of the global system. The fact that France's weight within the European Union will be reduced, and that a slow shift towards Central Europe will probably begin, in which cooperation between Germany and Central Europe (especially Poland) will have an enhanced role, is ultimately France's problem, and integration could even gain a new impetus. Europe as a whole will be weaker and will not be able to voice its opinion globally. It will have a lesser role in establishing universal rules to humanize global systems, which many of us believe to be the primary mission of Europe. Though the world may still be successful, especially in the Asian regions, the question remains will it not be poorer, especially as regards the values of our several-thousand-year-old civilization and the norms it gave rise to (true, out of "undue caution," it might have been wiser to refer to the source of these values and the values themselves in the Constitutional Treaty). [...]

We have to find the areas where the European project has been particularly successful, and this is basically in the area of economic integration and the legal regulation and legal culture that serve it. The debate on the socio-economic model ought to be continued, and it should be accepted that the historical and political traditions of Europe justify the existence of different economic and social models in parallel and in competition with each other, without prejudice to the identity of fundamental values. Different varieties of the classical and the neoliberal free-market model, the Rhine social-market-economy model, and the traditional statist-Colbertist model continue to exist side by side in European thought, and political ideologies and party interests sometimes sharpen the differences that result from the divergence of the original models. It must be accepted that no model can become exclusive in Europe, and in this area too it must be recognised that

Introduction

Europe's tradition, strength, and future lie in diversity, in dialogue, competition, and cooperation between colours.

This debate should also be continued with regard to the political institutional system. Europe's mission is not only to make the global system more humane and just but probably also to renew the institutions of mass democracy. Slogans increasingly far-fetched and unrealistic, the growing role of political communication and marketing, and the general decline in the quality of the media will not help renew democracy. Above all, Europe needs values and a renewed understanding of human rights, and it needs to realize that a modern society can only function democratically if subsidiarity is genuinely applied, and that people are not only individuals but also personalities, and that they acquire and fulfil their personalities by belonging to a community. Renewal will not be easy, but perhaps it will not take fifty years.[10]

All this history is now. Or is it not? Most of the content of the rejected Constitutional Treaty was preserved as an amendment to the Founding Treaties, and this was how the Lisbon Treaty was adopted and came into force in 2009. This outcome was largely enabled by the committee (the drafter of the new Founding Treaty) organized and chaired by the former vice-president of the Convention, Giuliano Amato,[11] and the incoming German presidency, which, due to the Dutch opposition, finally resolved the dispute by the legal technique of treaty amendment. For all the difficulties, the process of European integration continued; it overcame the financial crisis that turned into a sovereign debt crisis, though many of the difficulties were caused by the errors of its own monetary and fiscal policies. The real challenge, however, was not the crisis itself, but the increasingly obvious imbalance among three areas: an undoubtedly successful economic integration (though threatened by the fragility of the euro), the very limited success of political union, and the serious shortcomings of the cultural dimension. It was in view of this imbalance

---

[10] Martonyi, János, "Hogyan tovább, Európa?" In idem., *Mi és a világ*. Budapest, Magyar Szemle Alapítvány, 2015, 275–280; see also idem, "Hogyan tovább, Európa?" *Heti Válasz*, volume 5 (2005), number 22, 55–57.

[11] The members of the Action Committee for European Democracy (ACED) included Giuliano Amato, Michel Barnier, Stefan Collignon, Jean-Luc Dehaene, Danuta Hübner, Sandra Kalniete, Wim Kok, Paavo Lipponen, János Martonyi, Inigo Mendez de Vigo, Chris Patten, Otto Schily, Costas Simitis, Dominique Strauss-Kahn, António Vitorino, and Margot Wallström.

Introduction

and, above all, the need to strengthen the cultural dimension, i.e., European identity, that three years ago I proposed:

> Let us rediscover identity. European identity, European culture, European civilization, our being, our roots, our nature, and our being unto ourselves. Many people seem to be in need of this discovery. And if we have discovered it, then this cultural-civilizational dimension, this European identity, must be placed at the heart of the European project. There is no problem with our not seeing eye to eye on the individual content elements of this identity. In his speech referred to and delivered at the Sorbonne, President Macron failed to see Notre Dame a mere five- or six-hundred metres away, and all he could think of when listing the criteria of European identity was the Greek temples. He was right, because the heritage of antiquity is undoubtedly a very important foundation of Europe. But not to see Notre Dame from the Sorbonne, not to see the Dome in Cologne, or not to see St Peter's Cathedral is a mistake we cannot condone. If we forget one of the most important foundations of European identity, it will be difficult to keep Europe and the European Union together. We respect *laïcité*, we understand that it is a very important shaping factor in French history. We also respect and accept the Enlightenment and its values. European history would be different without the Enlightenment, and Europe would not be what it is. And the principles of freedom, equality, and fraternity, as well as their defence, are particularly important today. Most importantly, all these values together have shaped European identity; for some people one element is more important than the other, but European identity cannot do without its cultural and spiritual heritage. Without rediscovering and reinforcing this cultural and civilizational dimension, we will not be able to move forward, even if we come up with the most ingenious, clever and innovative economic, financial, and legal solutions.[12]

As to the present, this volume contains an essay I wrote on the occasion of the 70th anniversary of the Schuman Declaration, in which I attempt to

---

12   Martonyi, János, "Változatok az európai integráció jövőjére". In idem., *Nyitás és identitás*, Szeged, Pólay Elemér Alapítvány, 151–156, the edited version of a lecture delivered at the conference organized by the Faculty of Law of the University of Szeged, 23 September 2017.

Introduction

give a possible interpretation of the concepts of nation and federalism, which I have been advocating for decades and have never given up. Nothing has changed or will change my mind on this, not the reassessment of de Gaulle's Europe policy nor the growing animosity to European integration on both the Right and the Left. One of the reasons for this is my vision of Europe based on the gradual and balanced realization of European integration based on an existing European identity, which, though, is secondary to national identities; and another equally important reason is that European integration based on the cultural concept of nation, a supra-state Europe of nations, is a fundamental Hungarian national interest.

Neither the cultural nation (that being defined as a historical, linguistic, cultural, spiritual community) nor true federalism (that based on the recognition of the identity of free, bottom-up linguistic and cultural communities, their collective rights and thus their autonomy) is a matter of "real time," one that can be realized in the near future. Yet, the future of European integration will largely hinge on the success—or failure—of linking the cultural concept of nation and bottom-up historical federalism. The successes and failures of seventy years and the recurring and increasingly permanent challenges and crises of recent years now suggest that the way forward is to move beyond the traditional and increasingly sterile debates, the power or competence struggles masked as continuous institutional reform, and to dig deeper to find the possibilities of renewing European integration.

A new impetus requires new approaches, for example, a new approach to integration, which would better reflect Europe's historical characteristics, more effectively realize its diversity, more fully recognize the autonomy of linguistic and cultural communities, and create democratic legitimacy based on subsidiarity. However, the international-law basis cannot but continue to be the decision of the sovereign Member States to entrust the exercise of part—but only part—of their rights arising from their sovereignty (in other words, they do not relinquish their sovereignty) to the common EU institutions and to exercise these competences jointly by way of these institutions. (This decision can moreover be revoked by announcing the intention to leave.) State sovereignty is the indispensable legal basis for integration as a whole, which is not weakened but strengthened by the recognition of linguistic, cultural, and spiritual communities, just as the recognition of the existence of these communities and the consequences to be drawn thereof would strengthen the European institutions.

Introduction

One of the often-mentioned dilemmas of European integration is the imbalance among the economic, political, and cultural dimensions of integration. Strengthening the role of linguistic and cultural communities could give a local and all-European impetus to the cultural dimension, which has been marginalized until now. A European identity cannot be created by the single market alone, the successful and strong common currency, or even increased financial transfers. To do this, we need to go back to our roots, to our common "Three Hills," to our common history, which is both local and European. The essence of the latter is diversity, which is the greatest advantage of what Robert Schuman called *espace de civilization* over other cultures. If this be the case, not only must we accept ideological differences within this civilizational space, but we must also give linguistic and cultural communities a greater role than they have hitherto had. The way to strengthen European identity is through a primary community identity, i.e., a national identity based on linguistic, cultural, and spiritual community, and this requires that the concept of nation also be approached from primarily a cultural perspective.

Strengthening national and European identities together would make a significant contribution to alleviating the multiple divisions within the European Union. Today, divisions arise not only from economic and financial interests and the corresponding views on economic policy but also from deeper historical, cultural, and related ideological and values issues. Recognizing diversity based on linguistic and cultural community identities could mitigate the unconditional belief in the exclusive correctness and moral superiority of a political ideology based on a particular world view and the political intolerance it generates.

Once again, Jean Monnet's oft-quoted dictum that the process of European integration is "forged in crises" has been proven right. The pandemic and the unpredictable economic crisis it has given rise to—multiply more severe than the 2008 crisis—have made joint action inevitable and forced divisions to be overcome between, above all, North and South. It was not easy, but we succeeded in no more than five days. A number of factors not analyzed here played a role in achieving it, the process leading to it having been under way for some time; yet, without the shock of the pandemic, the decisions would not have been taken. The tools of monetary policy were exhausted; the experience of the 2008 crisis had made it abundantly clear that fiscal austerity would do more harm than good; extraordinary instruments and deci-

Introduction

sions were needed in the emergency; and the primary responsibility for joint action in the face of an existential threat to integration lay with the Member States. The large states were first, with the least inclined following suit. Member States understood that preserving the unity of the internal market and reducing market distortions due to diverging levels of state aid required more decisive and swifter action than ever before.

Oddly enough, action was also assisted by the latest developments in the decades-long dispute over competence between the European Court of Justice and the constitutional courts of the Member States, the *Bundesverfassungsgericht* of Germany in particular. The ruling of the German Constitutional Court in the PSPP case (5 May 2020) demonstrated, among other things, that there are limits to the common monetary policy and the instruments that can be used to implement it, that monetary policy is closely linked to fiscal and economic policy, and that the Member States cannot be circumvented in the latter area. The monetary policy options of the European Central Bank are not unconstrained insofar as the instrument concerned has fiscal and economic policy consequences, and the Court of Justice of the European Union should therefore have perceived the lack of conferral of competence and, consequently, democratic legitimacy. In order to prevent the *Bundesverfassungsgericht* from delivering another similarly negative judgment on the even more substantial ECB bond-purchase programme necessitated by the pandemic, the EU Member States themselves—by way of the highest-level institution of integration—made the decision on a one-off fiscal measure of a huge sum and vast importance, thereby resolving the dispute over competence or at least postponing it to the next round. Whether this is a one-off decision, or whether another exceptional situation will require another similar decision remains to be seen. In any event, no new system was created, and no Eurobond was introduced, as many had been demanding for decades; what was decided upon was a one-off borrowing, considered exceptional.

The general state of integration, the concerns and uncertainties about the euro, the experience of the crisis a decade ago, the exhaustion of monetary policy options, the political and legal debates between Member States and the integration institutions on national sovereignty, the scope and exercise of conferred competences, and the limits of the primacy of European law all pointed in the same direction. Had the Member States been unable to take swift and decisive action in the given situation, the entire integration process might have been jeopardized, the euro collapsed, the single internal market disintegrated, and the debates running throughout the process on the fundamental nature of integration might have become uncontrollable, with all the political, institutional, and legal consequences.

Arguably, well-nigh probably, all this would not have been enough to bring about the decision to substantially change the German position, to table the Franco–German initiative, to convince the Frugal Four, or even to interpret the Treaties in an undoubtedly reasonable yet flexible manner. But then come the pandemic, and with it the threat and even the reality of an unforeseeable economic crisis. Monnet was right: European integration is forged in crises.

Once the otherwise justified celebration ends, we need to grasp that though the agreement that the European Council reached (thanks to the many factors mentioned, the launching of Next Generation EU in particular) does indeed make a significant contribution to overcoming the current crisis, it does not resolve all the dilemmas of integration or exclude future challenges or even crises. The elements of permanence are borne not only by the world but by European integration as well, and not only in its fundamental values and impressive results but also in its contradictions.

Unresolved from the outset, the question concerning the fundamental nature of integration, its status in international law, which is closely linked to the dispute over sovereignty, remains open. Is the European Union an international organization or a (quasi) federal state? There is now perhaps a consensus that it is neither, and the prevailing view is that the Union is a *sui generis* organization and cannot be considered a mere international organization, but it is certainly not a federal state, not even a confederation. The *sui generis* designation is an attractive theoretical solution, but it cannot provide clear answers to a number of questions. In particular, there is no answer to the question whether European law is a system of rules established by a traditional international organization, which must be fully integrated into international law, or whether it is the autonomous legal order of an evolving federal state ("ever closer union"). A further, more important and controversial question is whether EU law has absolute and unconditional supremacy over the laws of the Member States, or whether this doctrine, developed by the European Court of Justice, can be limited in certain cases by the Member States through their constitutions or their constitutional courts. These limits were also established by case law, though not that of the European Court

Introduction

of Justice but that of the constitutional courts of the Member States. Started by the *Bundesverfassungsgericht*, the process of defining these limits began with the protection of fundamental rights and then turned to the constitutional identity of the Member States, and later went on to frame the broader and more sensitive *ultra vires* thesis, the essence of which is that EU institutions are not to go beyond the limits of the competences conferred upon them by the sovereign Member States.

The notion of constitutional identity is based on concept of national identity, which is provided for by the Treaties (Article 4(2) TEU), as is the notion of the conferral of competences in three different formulations (Articles 4(1), 5(1), and 5(2) TEU). There is no general definition of the scope of constitutional identity (nor is there a clear one of the concept of national identity); the Member States define it only in regard of themselves, their own constitutional identity, through their constitutions or constitutional courts, and, naturally, its scope may vary from one Member State to another and also over time. The essential question, however, remains the same: Where is the borderline between the constitutional core of the legal order of the Member States and the primacy of European law; where is the line protecting the sovereignty of the Member States beyond which the primacy of European law does not prevail? Constitutional identity has by now become the subject of considerable literature, both international and Hungarian, and numerous international conferences. Currently, their main message is that both the European Court of Justice and the constitutional courts of the Member States need to show reasonable restraint and mutual respect, which must be grounded on and accompanied by impartial and balanced dialogue both in academia and case law. In importance, the issue points far beyond the dilemma of the conflict between the two levels of norms and represents one of the general theoretical and political dilemmas in the development of integration.

The same fundamental issue comes up in the *ultra vires* thesis, with the difference that here we are dealing with a much more complex, deep-rooted, and unresolvable conflict. No purely logical method or legal interpretation can unravel it. The gist of it is the following: as per the principle of conferral of competences repeatedly laid down by the Treaty, a sovereign State confers on EU institutions the exercise of those of its competences the Treaty defines, and the source of the decision by the State is, in principle, its unlimited (in practice, limited) sovereignty. This sovereignty is not lost, nor is it constrained,

Introduction

as the conferral of competences can be revoked at any time by withdrawal from the Union.

Within the scope of the conferral of competences (but only within it), the primacy of European law prevails, and the European Court of Justice has exclusive jurisdiction to interpret and apply European law (Article 19(1) TEU, second sentence). It is logically impossible to decide who is ultimately entitled to establish whether or not a conferral extends to a particular matter because the decision on the conferral was brought by the sovereign while the competence is exercised jointly by the sovereigns through their common institutions. If, for example, an EU institution manifestly exceeds the competences conferred upon it, the sovereign is entitled to object that it did not confer the exercise of the competence concerned. If, however, the Member States were to have the final say on the scope of that competence, it would be impossible to establish uniformly the scope of Community, and later EU, competence, because the courts of the twenty-seven Member States—rather than a single European Court of Justice—could decide differently on the precise scope of the conferral. There is therefore no purely legal solution, the starting point having to be clearly defined as a precondition of the decision.[13]

Again, the only way out is cooperation based on mutual respect and common sense. The first condition of this is that the EU institutions abstain from using the creeping extension of competences, and that the Commission does not initiate adoption of new legal mechanisms or regulations that have no legal basis in the Treaties or are even contrary to primary EU law. Nevertheless, should an EU act clearly contravene the *ultra vires* prohibition and not be perceived by the European Court of Justice, it would be difficult to dispute the recent ruling of the German *Bundesverfassungsgericht* that such an act lacks the minimum democratic legitimacy required by the *Grundgesetz*, does not respect the basis of division of competences, and undermines the principle of conferral of competences, which is a fundamental principle of the European Union.

However, the ruling of the German Constitutional Court in the PSPP case also illustrates the theoretical and practical uncertainty concerning the

---

13 Jakab, András and Pál Sonnevend, "The Bundesbank is under a legal obligation to ignore the PSPP Judgment of the Bundesverfassungsgericht." https://verfassungsblog.de/the-bundesbank-is-under-a-legal-obligation-to-ignore-the-pspp-judgment-of-the-bundesverfassungsgericht/

Introduction

application of the prohibition on exceeding competence. The reasoning of the judgment is convincing in principle, and it ultimately finds the political and legal basis of control by the Member States of the competence conferred to the EU institutions. However, it is far from clear that the principles were tenable and applicable in the specific case. Opinions differ on this point. In the PSPP case, the European Central Bank was found to have exceeded its competence by failing to carry out the proportionality assessment that it was to have in the context of the division of competences. Although the ECB implemented the PSPP programme under the monetary policy conferred onto EU institutions, it failed to take into account the impact of monetary instruments on fiscal and economic policies, which were not within EU competence. The ECB thus breached the prohibition of *ultra vires,* and the European Court of Justice failed to carry out a review that would have been necessary to establish this exceeding of competence, and thereby the Court itself crossed the *ultra vires* limit.

Even without a detailed analysis of the judgment, it can be concluded that the competence to establish competence (*Kompetenz der Kompetenz*) raises not only theoretical but also serious practical problems. The distinction between monetary and fiscal policy is not always clear-cut, especially in a situation where monetary policy also tries to supplement fiscal instruments, which increasingly exhausts the monetary toolbox, and it gradually becomes clear that fiscal instruments are also needed. By way of legal dispute over the division of competences, the German judgment highlighted the close relation between monetary, fiscal, and economic policies, and that, if fiscal action is needed, it is to be decided by the Member States. There will be much debate on the ruling and its implications—its future consequences—but it is perhaps possible that, in addition to the crisis caused by the pandemic, the *Bundesverfassungsgericht* also contributed to the great turnaround of the German position during the emergency, and indirectly contributed to Member States finally agreeing to launch Next Generation EU and allow the joint borrowing required to do so.

The relationship between EU law and national laws can therefore no longer be reduced to the absolute primacy of EU law. The doctrine of constitutional identity has been brought up and applied in several Member States, but its scope varies from one Member State to another and cannot be precisely defined. In addition, Member States will likewise apply the prohibition on exceeding competences, with all the legal and political consequences this entails. There are, and will therefore be, no clear and universally accepted boundaries between the regulatory and judicial decision-making competences of the EU and the Member States, and the clashes between levels are a permanent feature of the integration process. This is a natural consequence of the *sui generis* nature of the European Union as an integration organization, which simultaneously implies the primacy and autonomy of EU law and the preservation of the sovereignty of the Member States, and that the Member States jointly exercise the competences deriving from their sovereignty that the Treaties define.

However, the dilemmas and debates about the relationship between the regulatory and decision-making levels are not limited to the relationship between the EU and national levels. Similar issues arise in the relationship between international law and EU law. The common root of both dilemmas is that the place of European law is not clearly defined in the universal hierarchy of legal norms, which in turn, as we have seen, is ultimately a consequence of the fact that the legal nature of the European Union is not clearly defined, and we do not know exactly what is meant by the *sui generis* designation.

This is the fundamental reason why the relationship between international law and European law is one of the most often discussed topics in the legal literature and a recurrent issue in the case law of the European Court of Justice. The European Union has legal personality, and, as a subject of public international law, it is obliged to respect both international treaties and customary international law. The international agreements it concludes are binding on its institutions and Member States (Article 216(2) TFEU). The European Union itself was established by international law, and the treaties thereof as primary Union law are themselves part of international law, which is undergoing a process of increasing fragmentation and pluralization. The European Union is therefore not only subject to international law but is also a shaper of and contributor to its development. The contribution is rather important: its legal institutions and rules serve as a model for multilateral and universal legal norms; indeed, it is a laboratory of universal rule-making.

The international agreements concluded by the European Union become part of its legal order, implying that these are not only directly applicable but also have direct effect, so that legal entities can rely on them directly before national and EU institutions, including the courts. However, this direct effect has never been absolute and automatic. The case-law of the European Court

Introduction

of Justice has established two requirements of direct effect. The first one is that "the nature and the broad logic" of an agreement does not preclude direct effect, and the second is that the content of the provision invoked must be "unconditional and sufficiently precise."[14] The enforcement of these requirements led to a gradual narrowing of the scope of direct effect. The doctrine of the autonomy of European law has also been increasingly applied to secondary EU law. In the case of primary law, the European Court of Justice has made it clear that the primacy of international agreements does not extend to primary EU law, "in particular to the general principles of which fundamental rights form part." In its next ruling, the ECJ set an even stricter limit by stating that international law can only be applied (permeate the autonomous European legal order) if it is in line with the conditions created by the basic principles of European law.[15] In these judgments, the ECJ essentially marked out the place of European law in the hierarchy of norms by raising primary law and rules expressing basic constitutional principles above international law (except for *ius cogens* rules), and, as regards secondary law, it recognized the primacy of international law without prejudice to the fundamental principles of European law. This conclusion and practice are based on the autonomy of the European legal order, which must be respected not only in the field of fundamental rights but also in other areas, such as investment protection conventions.

It would be difficult to miss the clear link between European law and the laws of the Member States on the one hand and international law and European law on the other. Invoking their constitutional identity and the prohibition of *ultra vires*, the Member States have set up barriers to the unconditional and absolute primacy of European law, and, particularly by way of their constitutional courts, will not relax these barriers in the future. On the basis of the autonomy of the European legal order, the European Court of Justice has

---

14   Judgment of 4 February 2016, *Joined Cases C-659/13 and C-34/14, C & J Clark International*, ECLI:EU:C:2016:74, cited in Allan Rosas, *The European Court of Justice and Public International Law*, CAHDI, Strasbourg, 23 March 2018, https://rm.coe.int/statement-delivered-by-judge-allan-rosas-at-the-55th-cahdi-meeting-55t/16807h3h04 (accessed 29 September 2020); see also Blutman, László: *A nemzetközi jog érvényesülése a magyar jogban: fogalmi keretek*. MTA Doctoral Thesis, Szeged, 2015, 97–99.

15   Judgment of 3 September 2008, *Joined Cases C-402/05 P and C-415/05 P, Kadi v. Council and Commission (Kadi)*, ECLI:EU:C:2008:461. Katja Ziegler, "Autonomy: From Myth to Reality - Or Hubris on a Tightrope? EU Law, Human Rights and International Law." In Sionaidh Douglas-Scott, Nicholas Hatzis (eds.), *Research Handbook on EU Law and Human Rights*, Edward Elgar Publishing, 2017, 295.

raised primary European law (which is itself international law) above international law, and it only recognizes the primacy of international law subject to strict limitations, even in respect of the secondary law EU institutions adopt. Thus, no pure hierarchy of norms applies in either context. There is a system (*ius cogens,* primary European law, international law, secondary European law, and the laws of the Member States), but there is no clear and unambiguous hierarchy. That is why we might call this system—borrowing a term from brain science, informatics, and geopolitics—a heterarchy instead of a hierarchy.

The geometric structure of legal norms is thus shifting from hierarchy to heterarchy. One—but not the only—reason for this is the emergence of European integration and thus of an autonomous level of Community, later EU, law, which takes precedence over the law of the Member States, but sovereign states cannot subject their constitutional core and identity to secondary European law. By the same token, primary EU law, as the basis of an autonomous European legal order, can only accept the binding force of public international law subject to limitations. As the scope of the limitations actually applied is clearly and precisely defined neither in the case of international law nor in the case of the primacy of European law, inevitable conflicts arise between levels of regulation and decision-making, some even note a "battle of tribunals." This is not conducive to the universal rule of law and legal certainty. But these conflicts are far from being confined to the field of law, nor do they originate there. In fact, they are the inevitable consequences of the increasing complexity, unpredictability, and disorder that characterize the world's overall economic, geopolitical, social, and institutional developments.

The first chapter of *We and the World,* the collection of my essays published between 2002 and 2010, is entitled "People." What the people I profile—Pope John Paul II, Ferenc Mádl, Mikhail Gorbachev, Sándor Csoóri, Árpád Fasang, Sándor Kiss (Alexandre Kiss), Miklós Kun, and Ferenc Borbíró—all have in common is that they have contributed to making the world a better place. Some made the whole world better, and some did the same through their nation in public life, literature, science, or even in running a small town and upholding its Hungarian identity. By simultaneously improving the world and keeping a strong sense of community identity, they helped the world by belonging to the community.

The list of names is largely accidental, as most of the speeches, addresses or tributes I agreed to deliver were occasioned by invitation and the subjects

Introduction

were not my choice. That is how these commemorations were incepted, and how they came to be included in that book. Nevertheless, the list is united by the fact that no person is truly successful without belonging to a community, without a community identity, for only those that live and work for the well-being not of themselves but of their community can be truly successful. It is these people's sense of individual identity that creates, maintains, and strengthens community identity, without which there would be no lasting communities, no churches, no nations, no history, and the world would have fallen apart long ago. But it has not fallen apart, and it will not fall apart; strong communities, and, above all our nation, will remain, regardless of how community identity is currently branded, and how, in its extreme forms, it can be and has been distorted.

Openness and Identity, the volume of my essays written between 2014 and 2018, does not include chapters on persons as the previous one did. The people in *We and the World* presented, as it were, the essence and roots of identity, the main theme of the first chapter of that book. In the introduction to *Openness and Identity*, I wrote that some "simultaneously believe in the need for a community identity, especially national identity, in the shared responsibility to preserve and transmit the historical and cultural heritage that underpins it, and in the need to open up to the world, in a free, fair and rules-based world trade, in the possibility of humanizing global processes and imbuing them with universal moral content."

The *Tributes* chapter of this volume continues the series about people. In the order in which they were written, they are about Géza Herczegh, Tom Lantos, József Antall, János Horváth, and Otto von Habsburg. Again, the list was compiled by factors outside my control. By coincidence? Perhaps, but coincidence—or what appears to be coincidence—plays a very important role in our lives and in history. One has to trust it, because coincidence compiled the list in a spirit of continuity and on the basis of the same criteria as the previous one. The tributes themselves describe individual features of the persons and the differences between them. What is common to each is an identity that is both national and European; their responsibility for each other, for the nation, for the country, for the world; their concern for universal and European values, for service to the nation at the highest level, in different situations and in changing circumstances, but with similar commitment; and their linking of the global and the local, and their embrace,

Introduction

pursuit, and fulfilment of both the dictums "every Hungarian is responsible for every Hungarian" and "every person is responsible for every person" in their lifework.

In the same vein, the tributes are also about Hungarians who rescued, took care of, and schooled French prisoners of war who fled to us during the most dire years of World War II and bore witness to universal human values and solidarity; Hungarians who fought one of the greatest struggles for freedom in European history in 1848/49, and who did so much for human freedom and national independence; Hungarians who preserved the unity of their nation in the hundred years that followed, even though their country was dismembered in a way unprecedented in history. The commemorations were delivered in a variety of venues, from the French Institute in Budapest to Sepsiszentgyörgy (Sfântu Gheorghe, Romania), and Szada in Hungary. Coincidence worked well here too, and no one could have linked the universal with the national, the wider world with what we call home so well—no one except the one who placed coincidence into the great system he created.

This volume also follows on from the previous ones in that, after presenting people and events preserving and symbolizing our community identity, it opens up to the world, attempting to explore some of the more important elements of the rapidly changing and increasingly interconnected realities of geopolitics and world trade.

Commercial policy, or foreign economic policy in the broadest sense, has always been an important area of international relations and the promotion of the interests of sovereign states within them. This policy is therefore part of state economic policy, including monetary policy (customs revenue), industrial policy (industry protection), agricultural policy (market protection and export subsidies), and foreign policy pursuing geopolitical objectives. Foreign economic policy and foreign policy are part of the same state policy, they should pursue a single set of goals and mutually support each other. However, foreign economic policy has always had its own set of instruments and relative autonomy, and economic and trade interests have not always concurred with geopolitical aims and interests. In recent years, the traditional instruments of commercial policy have increasingly become instruments of foreign policy, as it were, dissolving into geopolitics. A related dilemma of international commercial policy is that, as it has had a well-developed and relatively well-functioning regulatory and a more or less respected dispute settlement

Introduction

system, expectations of it have been set enormously high. These expectations are understandable and to a large extent justified, since trade and its regulation are now inseparable from the environment and its protection, and even the most perfect environmental and commercial regulation is questionable if it ignores fundamental human values and rights. But their interconnectedness should not be a reason to place the burden of all global challenges on trade regulations and the dispute settlement procedures that build on them. For all their relative sophistication, these regional and multilateral arrangements will not be able to resolve all the world's problems. As much as it is reasonable to correlate, for example, climate-change requirements, fundamental human rights values and standards, and trade and economic regulations, it is impossible to expect trade agreements to shoulder the burden and solve the problems of all other areas. Indeed, excessive expectations and requirements can lead to the collapse, or at least stall the development, of an overburdened trade-regulation system, as has been the case in multilateral trading systems, largely due to the over-extension of the regulatory scope.

There are two threats to traditional commercial policy and the trade agreements that represent it. First, an increasingly intense geopolitical competition is resulting in tensions and conflicts, which places the entire toolbox of commercial policy in the service of geopolitics, depriving it of both the relative autonomy it previously enjoyed and the degree of stability and predictability provided by international law. Second, commercial regulation and dispute settlement are overburdened by issues that, appropriately, non-commercial policy areas should regulate and enforce within their own international legal regimes.

Both processes are based on understandable considerations, but if they go beyond what is reasonable, commercial policy will fail to fulfil its original function of developing and fairly regulating commercial relations between and among states. Nor will commercial policy be able to contribute effectively to geopolitical goals, nor can it give meaningful input to the protection of values beyond the economy. What is needed, therefore, is a balance between geopolitics and commercial policy on the one hand and between commercial-policy objectives and non-economic values on the other, which balance preserves the system that has worked so far and simultaneously takes reasonable account of the increasing interdependence of the different areas and the accelerating pace of change.

Introduction

The essence of the heterarchical structure is that different powers have dominant roles in diverse areas, and competition becomes increasingly keen not only within each area but also between them. Also, it is of consequence the tools of which area dominate a geopolitical confrontation. Commercial policy instruments may succeed or fail in competition, but it is better for the world to have geopolitical jockeying conducted through reciprocal tariff increases than through proliferating nuclear warheads or the threat to use them.

In the overall geopolitical competition, leadership in an area may change, as it has always changed. Culture is undoubtedly the most important factor of influence in all areas. The two areas that will determine the outcome of geopolitical competition in the longer term are demography and technology. Ultimately, both are part of the broader culture, civilization, and both are "decided in our minds."

Culture will likewise determine the future of Europe, and, within it, the European Union, which is the subject of the studies in the third part of this volume. Jean Monnet is credited with saying that, if the process of European integration were to be relaunched, it would have to start with culture. Monnet may or may not have said this, but certainly he could have. The saying clearly expresses the dilemma that the cultural dimension of integration has been relegated to the background, and that the elaboration and reinforcement of the components of European identity, including community identity, has lagged much behind economic and political integration. This is the main reason why a sense of community based on Europe's historical and cultural heritage and a corresponding sense of political belonging have not evolved. This has happened notwithstanding the fact that the Founding Treaties themselves stress the crucial role of culture in integration. Central Europe, the historical and cultural heritage of this region, is an indispensable element of this diverse but essentially and fundamentally single European culture. As I wrote twenty-seven years ago,[16] this region could give new impetus to European integration, which, struggling as it may with crises, is, on the whole, successful.

Szada, August 2020

---

16 "Közép-Európa és az európai integráció. *Európai Szemle*, volume 4 (1993), number 3, 3–23, also in Martonyi, János, *Európa, nemzet, jogállam*. Budapest, Magyar Szemle – Európai Utas, 1998, 13–53.

Part I
Tributes

International Law, European Law, Hungarian Law

Delivered at a Memorial Conference on the occasion of the 90th anniversary of the birth of Géza Herczegh at the Faculty of Law and Political Sciences of the University of Pécs, 19 October 2018.[1]

Dear Melinda, dear Zsóka,[2] dear Dean, dear Friends,

I welcome you all with great respect and love; thank you very much for the invitation and the opportunity. First of all, I would like to apologize for a bit of a ruse. I gave a title to my speech for today, but that is not what I am going to talk about. In the interim, I made up my mind and decided I would rather speak about Géza Gábor Herczegh himself instead. As regards the subject matter mentioned—I mean the original title I gave and many things beyond— I would like to talk about someone I feel is a seminal figure in the Hungarian study of international law, Hungarian science, Hungarian historiography, Hungarian thought, Hungarian culture, Hungarian public life, and now we can safely say: Hungarian history, too.

Of course, we always say about him that he was an expert on international law and also an historian, but I think the point is more than that; he pursued the whole, not just the part. Behind international law, he saw and grasped the

---

[1] Published as "Köszöntő" (Welcoming address) in Béli, Gábor, and Bence Kelemen Kis, Ágoston Mohay and Szalayné Erzsébet Sándor (eds.), *Emlékkötet Herczegh Géza születésének 90. évfordulója alkalmából,* Pécs: PTE ÁJK Európa Központ, Publikon, 2018.
[2] Mrs. Géza Herczegh née Melinda Petneházy and Erzsébet Szalayné Sándor.

world in its entirety, the wider picture. He understood world politics—geopolitics, as we call it nowadays—, the larger economic context, and he had a bent for social policy. He never wanted to be directly involved in politics—he was wiser than that—but he did speak out from time to time. I would like to recall to you one of his contributions, because I found it particularly memorable. In 1994, he published an article[3] (Lady Melinda will remember) ... well, it was the day before the elections in 1994 that he had his thoughts appear in *Magyar Nemzet*—if interested, you might read it for yourselves—but, apart from that, he never would intervene in daily political life. As I said, he was interested in all the areas I listed, but, of course, most importantly, he understood and saw that the essence of the world is cultural above all. Though defined by many factors, and although different philosophies capture different factors, the world is primarily defined by culture. And culture is defined by cultural heritage. And cultural heritage cannot be understood without history. This understanding led him to his interest in history, to his works in that field, which I think are unique and enduring.

As an expert on international law, was he a realist or an idealist? I define Géza Gábor Herczegh as a realist driven by values. He was perfectly aware of the serious limits to international law. Yet, he also knew that international law has extraordinary capabilities. He also recognized the serious responsibilities international law bears. He was a freethinker on international law, but he also knew that there are more important things, values, influencing limits and capabilities. This is why he was a realist driven by values. He also had no doubt as to the source of values that have a universal and absolute nature. This was very important to him. But, of course, we still have not touched on the point that the deepest, strongest layer of his personality was his Hungarian identity. He was a Hungarian from Nagykapos [Veľké Kapušany, Slovakia].

Perhaps not "as Magyar, and as fugitive," but Herczegh could have said with Attila József that his "soul cries startled on," and implored "sweet Homeland, take me in your heart, let me be your faithful son!"[4] For he was truly a faithful son of his country—in Nagykapos, Budapest, Szeged, Pécs, The Hague and wherever else. It was also from the responsibility of international

---

3   Herczegh, Géza, "Téves képzetek rabságában. Elsodort nemzedékem". *Magyar Nemzet, 7 May* 1994. https://adtplus.arcanum.hu/hu/view/MagyarNemzet_1994_05/?pg=112&layout=s
4   "My Homeland", translation by Sándor Kerekes.

law that he derived, that he knew, that the only possible way to solve our national tragedy is rooted in law, international law, and human rights.

It was around this conviction that he built his oeuvre. He wrote about and spoke about it even when the direct subject matter of his writing or speech was something else, but it was always present. That is why he was truly a great Hungarian. Obviously, things change, and he could not live to see them, but he would certainly be needed today. Not so long ago, there was a similar commemoration at Pázmány Péter Catholic University, where I also spoke, delivering a scholarly lecture on—if my memory serves me—the different branches of international regulation, and I tried to compare and summarize them. I am thinking here of the regulation of world trade, particularly the world economy, issues of sustainability, and human rights, how to bring these three areas closer together and find the common principles on which to build them further. My original intention was to reflect on this, to approach the different levels of regulation, and to give a kind of analysis of these different levels of regulation, the geometry of law, as it were. That is what I am not doing now. Nevertheless, I do wish to point out that vast changes are taking place, and that the wisdom, serenity, moderation, impartiality, restraint, truthfulness, and, above all, of course, the strong Hungarian and moral commitment that Géza Gábor Herczegh stood for, are very much needed today and will be tomorrow.

In a nutshell, this is what I had intended to say, but I am not finishing just yet because we were also asked to recall personal experiences. I shall not run the gamut of my personal experiences because I would not meet the 15-minute time limit. The first time I visited Géza Gábor Herczegh I did not actually see him because he was not at home. He had left Szeged and no longer lived with Uncle László Tóth, his foster father, in the Arcade House. He was working at the Institute of Law in Budapest, but I kept hearing that Gábor was coming or not coming home on weekends. I never saw him, but I heard about him because his very kind and lovely sister, Aunt Klára, was my English teacher when I was eight or nine years old. Well, that was the beginning of my relationship with Géza Gábor Herczegh. Then, of course, a lot of other things happened, but I shall tell you about them next time. Just as the next time we have the opportunity I shall discuss the subject matter I mentioned.

Thank you very much for your attention!

Hungarian Foreign Policy, 896-1919
Reflections on Géza Herczegh's book

Delivered at the launch of the expanded edition of Géza Herczegh's Ma-
gyarország külpolitikája 896–1919 *(Budapest: Magyar Szemle, 2019), an event
organized by the Batthyány Lajos Foundation on 5 December 2019.*[1]

It would have been fortunate for me to have read this book before spending some decade and a half or two in active foreign policy. Let it be said in my favour that I had read the second volume, though I only now finished this first one. Better late than never. I fully agree that the sheer reading of this book is a matchless pleasure. Whether one is an expert on foreign policy or international law, a historian, or whatever else, this book is worth reading under any circumstances. In reviewing a book—if you can call it that—one might wonder whether to discuss primarily the author or the book. I would love to talk about the author on this occasion, but I spoke about him at a conference in Pécs not so long ago.

I said at that conference that Géza Herczegh "understood and saw that the essence of the world is cultural above all. Though defined by many factors, and although different philosophies capture different factors, the world is primarily defined by culture. And culture is defined by cultural heritage. And cultural heritage cannot be understood without history." And I added:

---

1 *Magyar Szemle*, new series, volume XXIX, 2020, numbers 1–2, 145–150.

As an expert on international law, was he a realist or an idealist? I define Géza Gábor Herczegh as a realist driven by values. He was perfectly aware of the serious limits to international law. Yet, he also knew that international law has extraordinary capabilities. He also recognized the stern responsibilities international law bears. He was a freethinker on international law, but he also knew that there are things, values, more important behind limits and capabilities. This is why he was a realist driven by values. ... For the deepest, strongest layer of his personality was his Hungarian identity. He was the Hungarian from Nagykapos [Veľké Kapušany, Slovakia]." Well, my dear friends, this book contains the very essence of the author, his Hungarianness. He clearly saw that without understanding external relations, the influence of external factors, it is impossible to understand Hungarian history and Hungary.

Lay people in particular often ask whether history could have been different. The conventional answer I think is no, because that was how it was. This is not true. It could have been different. It did not happen that way, it happened this way, but it could have happened otherwise. It could have happened differently because the world is not determined in every one of its elements and moments. Old Laplacean, all-encompassing, mechanical determinism should be forgotten. It follows, although science is only realizing it thanks to the twentieth century physicist Werner Heisenberg, that the world is subject to chance. He established the microphysical basis of chance, which applies to the whole system. The One that created this system thus put accidence into it. And if accidence is in the system, things could have been different. For example, external factors that were accidental compared to our system could have acted otherwise. In a philosophical sense, accidence is but the meeting, the intersection, of different causal processes. And history—I feel this comes through strongly in the book—is a series of coincidences. There are no closed systems. If there were, there would be no external influence, and, as thermodynamics suggests, a given system would turn into total disorder. But this is not case, because there is external energy and external action. Also, for example, there are values and principles, just as there is international law that intervenes. So, I think that, in retrospect, the past is the past, and it happened the way it happened. But in noting that the past could have happened differently, it is also easy to see that we can shape the present and the future. So, whoever made the system not only put accidence into it but also man with his free will and responsibility. The future can thus be shaped. All is not determined. The present and the future of this country can be shaped.

We often ask … indeed it is one of our recurring questions: What have we mucked up? How, when, and why did we muck it up? Who mucked it up? The simple answer is that we did not. We are here. We are still here after a thousand years. And we are here to stay. Of course, we have made many mistakes, just as others have made many mistakes, committed many sins. Let us not forget Radnóti's words, "we are guilty," but he went on to say, "as other peoples are.[2] We are no more or less guilty than other peoples. We are like other peoples.

Well, these questions do crop up. As a well-known saying has it, history repeats itself because we fail to learn from it. According to another version, history does not repeat itself because we learn from it. Foreign policy is something that can draw or tries to draw on many sciences or disciplines, but the true source of foreign policy cannot be anything other than history. Thus, we can learn from what has already happened in some way, we can draw conclusions from it, often perhaps even exaggerated conclusions because we believe that history repeats itself, but it never does, at least not in the way it happened originally. Nevertheless, history is what we can rely on. This is why I thought it would have been better for me to have read this book earlier, but it happened as it did.

Even belatedly, I think it is worth drawing some basic conclusions and formulating a few theses with a view to foreign policy. The first is that it is basically the competition, the struggle, between external and internal factors that governs the history of a country. A basic foreign-policy thesis is that the neighbourhood, the region, in which we live, is the most important factor. That the radius of foreign-policy action has expanded in recent times—call it globalization or whatever name you prefer—does not alter this: the most important factor remains the region. This is a fundamental thesis, and I think it was also an important recognition in our foreign policy that the relationship with our neighbours is of utmost importance. In our case, of course, this is particularly imperative because of the fate of the Hungarian nation. In any event, it is clear from the book that regional developments were what deter-

---

2   Miklós Radnóti, "I cannot know", translation by Gina Gönczi.

mined the country's destiny. It is also true, of course, that this book's coverage ends in 1919, and that the primary influence from the world outside Europe came thereafter; although the intervention of the United States in the First World War—again, an accidence—ultimately decided the fate of our country as well.

It all began with dynasties. A fascinating theme in the book is the relationship between dynasties and countries. Which was more important, dynasty or country? Both were important because a dynasty needed a country. A dynasty could increase its power by acquiring countries through marriage or war. Though this would increase either its economic or political clout, it was not yet clear whether it was in the interest of the country or the dynasty. As a matter of fact, foreign policy was almost a private affair of the dynast. He certainly treated it as such. For it was the dynast's business how his foreign relations, conquests, territorial losses, marriages, and adulteries affected the fate of his country. Foreign policy was therefore a private matter. Even today, there is a huge country where the debate is currently about whether foreign policy can be a private affair or exclusively a public affair. This is the question that Congress in Washington now needs to answer: Can foreign policy relations be used to further private ends? However thought-provoking, this question was not even raised in the age of dynasties. It was only natural that the ruler should pursue his own interests in foreign relations.

Dynasties determined the fate of countries. With the Árpád dynasty dying out, the history of our country was marked out by the rivalries and struggles of three or four Central European—again, the region is central—dynasties, the Jagiellons, Luxembourgs, Habsburgs, and Angevins, with the Habsburgs finally emerging as the strongest. However, they were not strong enough to defend the region against the new and formidable threat of the Ottoman Empire. For all its hereditary provinces, the House of Habsburg was unable to fend off such a powerful world empire.

And here comes the next big question, brought up throughout Hungarian history. What to do when a powerful force appears on the borders of the country. A force evidently much greater than its own. Many people today say that it would have been wiser to make our peace with the Turks. A well-known example is the case of the Romanian principalities, on which Béla Borsi-Kálmán has just published an excellent book. The Romanian principalities struck a compact with the Turks, and they may have fared better for it in the long run. Of course, there are other examples, like Bosnia. I am not at all sure Hungary would have come off well if it had reached an agreement with them at the price of 30 to 40 percent of its population converting to Islam, thus creating a rather peculiar society which would later be a source of grave problems. The dilemma of resistance, fighting, dying-in-arms or making peace, reconciliation, compromise, cooperation has remained with us. If only because one of the main characteristics of Hungarian historical writing is the search for the guilty and the traitors. It is no coincidence that those who advocated compromise would later be vilified as traitors. It is this particular scapegoating that is completely absent from Herczegh's book, because the author knew full well that this was not the point. But the question remains, whether to resist or to reach a compromise. Linked to this is the fundamental question of whether to proceed solely on the basis of realpolitik considerations or to adhere to certain fundamental values at the cost of heavy sacrifices.

This dilemma continues to be with us, and it was painfully sharp in Hungarian history just after the coming of the Turks. Regardless of the fact that we are not in the business of looking for scapegoats and determining where and when we mucked things up, in the period in question we gave the worst possible response to this dilemma of whether to resist, fight or reach a compromise. One part of us stood for resistance and the other for compromise. This divided the country in two in every sense of the word, not only politically, physically, and territorially but culturally too. Later, of course, we were split into three, which was one of the most tragic periods in Hungarian history. But the conclusion to be drawn from this is that there is nothing worse than division. In foreign relations, in foreign policy, what is categorically important is that whatever good or bad decision you come to, you must have the broadest possible national consensus behind it.

The author explains that dynasties had the great advantage that they provided continuity for as long as they lasted, as did the kings of the Árpád dynasty. However personal an affair foreign policy might have been, the mere existence of a dynasty lent a degree of continuity to the management of foreign relations and policy. Of course, a lot depended on marriages and so on, and a lot could change, but the dynasty itself meant continuity. And when this was interrupted in Hungarian history, when the Angevins could no longer hold on, bringing about dynastic rivalry, continuity ceased, and, continuity ceasing, national unity was in shambles. Continuity and consensus are thus closely related concepts. If there is continuity, there is consensus, and vice versa. With the dynasty dying out, continuity and consensus were gone. We split in two and had Ferdinand and John as pretenders to the crown, and so it continued for the next centuries under varying circumstances.

Should we choose Andrássy and Deák or Kossuth? Dualism or federalism? Dualism or unlimited national independence and sovereignty? We are still debating this today. Some stand for the Compromise, for accord. Essentially, I count myself among them. But I cannot say what would have happened if we had not chosen this path. Herczegh is apt to observe that Gyula Andrássy's foreign policy was the right foreign policy to follow at that time. Then, at that time. But Andrássy could hardly have known what would happen forty or fifty years later. Though in fact, he did foresee many things. For example, he was perfectly clear about the Russian threat. We had of course experienced it; it had been bloody concrete in 1849, and from that moment on it was obvious that we had to be part of a union of states in order to deal with the Russian threat in some way. We perhaps even managed the Russian threat for a while, but changes on the stage of world politics—the intervention of the United States of America that I just referred to—fundamentally altered the global geopolitical constellation. We suddenly found ourselves outside the region, beyond the North–South and West–East context, and we were confronted with a global factor that Deák and Andrássy could never have foreseen. Unforeseen, it was a development that can be regarded as accidence.

In fact, the nineteenth century saw the rise of a phenomenon that would determine our lives. The world was transforming. A new force appeared, and it seemed this new force, namely Germany, would reshape the destiny of Europe. There was no way of anticipating external, global developments with any degree of accuracy; no one would have expected that the foremost world power would do everything in its power to prevent this, even by war if necessary. Not by attacking Germany directly, British diplomacy was wiser than that. Rather, it sought to bring together a Franco–Russian alliance that would stop this rising power. This is what we call Thucydides' trap, in which a new power emerges, challenges the status quo, the existing system, and wants to take over, as did Germany, but in the end the defied power will not have it. That is what the First World War was about. And this brings us to the next big question: What should the power that is currently challenged by the rise of various new forces do to prevent this? This is the very question we are living. Herczegh's book cannot have dwelled on it. So now the question goes: By what means can the United States of America stabilize its challenged power, by what means can it stop, slow down or contain the rise of China? One thing is essential: that this should preferably not be done by means of war. This is also the most important lesson of the First World War.

I wished to refer to these among our dilemmas because I think the greatest strength of the book is that it shines with profound wisdom and is unbiassed. It is critical yet inoffensive. It is honest and accords responsibility its due place––always within sensible limits, of course. The book has, as I am inclined to have it, the calm serenity that characterized Géza Herczegh's whole personality. He expended an incredible amount of time, energy, diligent and thorough labour on this book. The serenity and calmness of his writing are assured by the qualities Herczegh possessed. Throughout his life but also in this book, he managed to avoid Hungarian, or, I should say, Central European, complexes. He suffered from no inferiority complex at all, neither at home nor in The Hague, nor anywhere else. We Central Europeans tend to be stricken with it. We can even be said to have—or to have had—a reason to feel inferior. But we must rid ourselves of it, not fall into its trap, and, above all, not try and compensate for it with a superiority complex. Because attempts have been and are being made to do so. This is wrong. Let us take a middle course, which is roughly the course this book takes, and which Herczegh followed all his life as a historian, as an expert on international law, and, above all, as a Hungarian.

These were the thoughts Géza Herczegh's book aroused in me. And lastly, a sentence that in itself could fully have done my job: make sure you read it, you will enjoy every word of it, and learn a great deal from it.

.

The Noble Banner of Human Rights

Presentation, at the book launch for The Noble Banner of Human Rights: Essays in Memory of Tom Lantos, *Hungarian Academy of Sciences, 31 January 2019*[1]

On this day we celebrate the launch of an excellent book, *The Noble Banner of Human Rights*, a testimony to the life, unique achievements, and first and foremost the outstanding legacy of an extraordinary person, statesman, thinker and friend of many of us in this room and well beyond in Hungary, the United States of America and across the world.

Who was he? It is hard to find the words for a perfect definition, if only because language is not the instrument through which we can express everything that is on our mind and in our soul. It is the nature of mysteries that they cannot be strictly identified, precisely because they are mysteries.

Hungarian by birth. American by choice. That is the slogan used in Tom's first race for Congress in 1980, as referred to in the wonderful essay by Robert R. King in this book. In fact, he was both Hungarian and American, in his heart and mind a Hungarian-American. But beyond these strong attachments, he was a deeply conscious member of a much larger community. He was a citizen of humankind.

However, to be a citizen of humankind, one needs to belong to smaller communities built upon one another. It is marvellously related in Katrina's

---

[1] Published in Anna-Maria Biro and Katrina Lanos Swett (eds.), *The Noble Banner of Human Rights, Essays in Memory of Tom Lantos*, Könyvbemutató, MTA, Budapest, 5–7.

53

Part I

Preface to the book how her dad told to his little girls about the „gradually growing concentric circles, spreading out from the centre" that is the family, „where our most important responsibility of love and support began." The widening circles—as he explained—represented the communities, the country, and finally the world.

Yes, that is the point where everything starts: a family man. „You cannot speak of Tom Lantos without speaking of Annette!" as Democratic Majority Leader Steny Hoyer said in the House of Representatives the day after Tom passed away—again as related in Robert's essay in the book. "Two people who became one, kindred spirits born of equal experience equally committed with a passion and a courage and an untiring commitment on behalf of those who needed a voice." The concentric circle of his family covered, of course, all those who came later. I shall never forget the lunch we had quite a while ago with his high-school-age grandson, Tomicah, whom he invited to join us to learn. It now looks like a successful idea.

A Hungarian by birth who never left Hungary in his heart. It was his country that cruelly left him in a crucial time. But later they met again, and he never lost his attachment to the collective identity of Hungarians represented by a historical heritage, a culture, a unique language that he so eloquently spoke. It was this particular attachment that was demonstrated by the tremendous help and support he gave to Hungary, to Hungarian minorities living in the neighbouring countries, and—put it simply—to Hungarians. But he was fully aware that there is an element of the general in any particular, just as—inversely—you cannot promote the general without acting on a particular issue. Human rights and freedoms are indivisible, fundamental values that cannot be selectively respected and cannot be variably treated depending on different historical or geographic situations.

He was a fighter, a "gallant warrior," as Katrina says in the Preface. One might say that in politics you are bound to be a fighter. But the real question is what you are fighting for and what you are fighting against.

Tom was fighting for freedom, human rights and dignity, democracy, the rule of law, the rights of the oppressed and the abused. He was fighting against defamation, denigration, degradation, discrimination, and double standards. He was fighting against racism and antisemitism in whatever form it might take. He was fighting for the good and fighting against the bad in all human beings. This is what made him a citizen of humankind.

He was also a rescuer. He escaped from victimhood and became a rescuer himself, helping the oppressed, the humiliated, and the excluded. He was a friend of those in need.

He was a friend of Hungary. A true friend in particular of those Hungarians who were and are in need. This is the primary reason why I want to convey the core of my message today in my former and present capacity. This is the message of gratitude.

I thank you, Tom, for defending my fellow Hungarians in Transylvania, where I myself happened to be born. I thank you for helping Hungarian minorities in all neighbouring countries. I thank you for what you have done for all minorities or oppressed communities in the world, as is well presented in the book we now launch.

I thank you Tom, for the way you received my apologies for what the Hungarian state did against and did not do for its, for our Jewish compatriots. I thank you for your watchful eye closely following the old-new risks and dangers in this field. Dangers that are also described in one of the thorough studies in the book.

From the long list of the actions you took in the interest of my country, Tom, I will now refer to only one, also because of the personal memory I carry. In 1999, March 12, we were flying to Independence, Missouri, to the Truman Library together with Madeleine Albright, Bronislaw Geremek, Jan Kavan, Géza Jeszenszky, and John Shattuck for the deposition there of the accession documents of Hungary, Poland, and the Czech Republic to NATO. And indeed this Washington to Independence flight was a journey back home. "Hungary has come home" and "We are back in the family," I said at that time, and Robert quotes me in his essay in the book.

However, without you, Tom, this memorable flight would not have taken place. Without your strong voice for expanding NATO, without your efforts and invaluable help, the accession of these three countries would not have happened at that time and in the same way. "I owe you a drink," I should say, but I cannot offer it to you, at least for the time being.

I started by referring to the celebration not only of the book, not even only of somebody we had the extreme privilege to have personal contact with, but also of his legacy. It is rooted in an unbelievably eventful and successful life, but it is for the future. A future full of uncertainties, risks, global and local challenges. We speak and write a lot about these risks and others, from climate change to artificial intelligence, from biotechnology to nuclear catastrophe. We should, I believe, do more. We need you, Tom, we need your vision, your commitment, your determination, your perseverance, your courage. Last, but not least, we need the basic and universal values you represented.

Acceptance Speech

Delivered at the presentation of the József Antall Prize at the Vigadó, Budapest, 16 May 2019.

Dear Friends,

Listening to the fine addresses, it occurred to me that, when honours and awards are presented, recipients' speeches tend to choose between two different options. I have attended a number of such ceremonies. The first option is for the recipient to enlarge on how much she or he did not deserve the award, how much more deserving others than herself or himself would have been. So far so good. The other option is somewhat more complicated, but there are examples of it: making a more nuanced and subtle, a more polished case, the recipient of the prize justifies why she or he actually deserved the prize, and why the person who most deserves it has now received it.

Well, I have heard many examples of both, but I do not wish to go either way now. Because they are both dull; because the real question is how such an award, such a distinction, affects the recipient. Calmly yet firmly, I dare say that this is the prize, this is the award that has affected me most profoundly all my life. In this context, I believe it is not the dwarfed dwarf who comes into the limelight but the person whose name this award bears. It is he I would like to say a few words about, even though my friend Gergely Gulyás has already done so. We have dwelled on him before, as others have done so too. Yet, I feel that this is an occasion when I must say a few words about him. To quote the poet, it is only now I see, now we see, what a giant he was.¹ No doubt we did see him that way, that we did feel and know that he was a prime minister of spirit, calm, serenity, and, yes, a sense of humour and moderation. We knew that he was a most outstanding Hungarian statesman in the twentieth century. We knew that he had a decisive role in the process of regime-change and transformation in Hungary and Central Europe, and a decisive role in launching Central European cooperation, which has since achieved extraordinary successes. He had a decisive role in disbanding the Easternist cooperation organizations. As we were wont to say, the Comecon and the Warsaw Pact were wound up without successors. And he also had a very important role in bringing about the process which—we hope—has culminated in the reunification of Europe.

Well, what I have to say here today is first a word of gratitude. I am deeply thankful for his having entered Hungarian and Central European history, indeed European history. From my point of view, perhaps most importantly, is that he entered my own life at a certain point and gave it a decisive turn. Many things could be cited, but perhaps the most important one is what my friend Gergely Gulyás has already mentioned, that he said (I am not quoting the first part of his sentence) that he considered himself the prime minister of 15 million Hungarians in spirit and sentiment. It is the precise essence of this sentence, that was misunderstood, that was bowdlerized, namely in spirit and sentiment. Because we are indeed Hungarians, but we are Hungarians first and foremost in spirit and sentiment. "Made Hungarian by reason, order, fate, intent, opportunity."² It is our spirit and sentiment that make us Hungarians. Today, we express this in a more complicated way, dwelling on identity, national self-identity. This is true enough, but it is all in our spirit and sentiment.

From a political point of view, these sentences and words were decisive, because they set in motion a process already well-known: the adoption of a new kind of regulation, under which we gave cross-border Hungarians various subsidies, entitlements, and benefits—causing no small controversy in neighbouring countries and further afield. The process continued, because a few years later, in 2010, we enabled those cross-border Hungarians whose fore-

---

1   The reference is to Attila József's poem "Mama."
2   A line from Endre Ady's poem "A tavalyi cselédekhez" (To Yesteryear's Maids).

bears lived not in present-day Hungary but in the historical territory of Hungary to acquire citizenship more easily. These are hugely important things in Hungarian national policy and in our lives, and I believe, without József Antall, without these words, none of this would ever have been achieved. Just as the reunification of Europe would not have come about the way it did. He captured the spirit and sentiment of the process, and then those that followed him worked to turn these ideas, ideals, and this spirit into reality. There were many people involved in this.

I would like to thank everyone here on this occasion too. Throughout these almost thirty years, there have been many joys and many trials. We did the job together, and I believe that such occasions as this one are particularly good for pointing out that we have ultimately achieved József Antall's fundamental ideas—the spirit and sentiment of the ideas—in terms of Hungarian national policy, launching cooperation in Central Europe, and our Europe policy. In fact, there is no other task than to work on fulfilling these objectives under different conditions, sometimes more, sometimes less difficult circumstances.

I therefore owe my gratitude first and foremost to József Antall and to those who made it possible for me to meet him. Here I must say a word about our mutual late friend György O'sváth, without whom this would not have happened. I also owe many thanks to all the colleagues I worked with then and in the decades that followed, and I am of course particularly grateful to the Board of Trustees, who thought—to take the first option after all—to give this year's prize to a man than whom anyone worthier would have been a good deal easier to find.

Thank you very much for your attention.

In memoriam János Horváth

Delivered at the János Horváth Memorial Conference *at the Petőfi Literary Museum, 21 January 2020.*[1]

The most important thing in any commemoration is what comes to mind first. More precisely, what one feels first. With János Horváth, I feel gratitude above all. I feel gratitude in the name of my country and my homeland, even in the name of the "free world," and of course in my own name. I learned a great deal from him: common sense—the common sense of the small-holder from the village of Cece—self-control, wisdom, impartiality, and, of course, uprightness and strength. Because he had plenty of it. We can all still learn from him. The other thing I feel, beyond thanks and gratitude, is pride. I am very proud that the accursed twentieth century also had its great Hungarians. Very great Hungarians. Indeed, even this much criticized past thirty years have also had their great Hungarians. János Horváth was one of them, he was a truly great Hungarian, and wherever he lived, whatever he did, he always bore witness to this special greatness of character, morality, and intellect.

One naturally thinks of personal experiences on such an occasion. When and how did I first meet him? Well, I met him relatively late, but still in time. It was in January 1990, in Indianapolis, where a memorable blue-ribbon committee was sitting. I am looking at Pál Márer—we are very glad you are here—

---

[1] Published in *In memoriam Prof. Dr. János Horváth 1921–2019. Emlékkonferencia, Budapest, 2020. január 21.* Budapest: Világörökségéért Alapítvány, 2020.

and Géza Jeszenszky, who were also there. In Indianapolis there was a very open, frank-faced, American-Hungarian professor who spoke Hungarian with the most Hungarian flavour possible. Moreover, he spoke a dialect, but I could not tell which one. I knew it was neither a Szeged nor a Hódmezővásárhely one, because that was what I knew and spoke. His was different, but indubitably Hungarian. Only a few hours later, I realized that he had the cadence of the same dialect in English; and then I remembered my father, who had a fair command of English but also the same peculiar Hungarian accent. Maybe that was how English was taught in the 1930s, but I think it was more than that for Hungarians living in America. This was one of their ways of preserving their Hungarianness, and János Horváth preserved his Hungarianness without a flaw.

What happened at that time is something I can never fail to bring to mind. He was the one who, in and around that very diverse blue-ribbon committee, introduced Hungarians to Hungarians, brought them together, tried to appease feuding homeland-Hungarians. He maintained his desire to pacify until the end of his life. He stood for the whole of Hungary, the entire homeland and nation. We have recalled his life story, and I do not wish to go back over it. Moreover, it could never be better put than Tibor Navracsics has just done. One thing is certain: no one knew the past hundred years of Hungarian history better than János Horváth did. He knew it, understood it, and what is more, he lived and shaped it. No one captured the essence of those three István Bibó years[2] as well as he did. Having lived those three years, he knew all too well that they concealed and encapsulated what would mature and unfold in the following forty years, his own history. He lived it so much that he was imprisoned at the end of 1947. Prison was not new to him, as he had been locked up by the Arrow Cross, escaping by the skin of his teeth. In this, too, he symbolizes Hungarian history and fate. He was needed, and so he left for America. He had a mission, a task, that was why he went. As fate would have it, he stayed on and continued to work in the States for the freedom of his country until his return late in his life.

Another personal memory is when he told me about American political indifference to the Hungarian uprising in 1956, bringing up the example of

---

2   1945–1947, the attempt to set up and hold on to democracy under the constant threat of communist takeover. A seminal political theorist, István Bibó wrote up the predicaments of those years in memorable essays.

Part I

US senators telling him that they were not going to endanger the security of the United States of America for a few hot-headed Hungarian youths. And indeed, the security of the world was not to be put at risk. But it could not have occurred even to those senators that the United States of America would never have won the Cold War the way it did without those few hot-headed Hungarian lads. Because it was these unruly youths who started the process that would ultimately lead to 1989, 1990, and 1991. It was much to the credit of, among many others, János Horváth, the many "János Horváths." As mentioned, he came back home in 1997. Many more of his kind should have! Not everyone could return, many had passed away. Many were elderly. Yet, some did come back. But no one helped as much as János Horváth. The Good Lord gave him the physical and spiritual ability to work even longer for his country. Had more of his kind come home, these past decades could have turned out better or even more successful.

János Horváth was one of the most active members of the Parliamentary Committee on Foreign Affairs. This committee heard me on several occasions, and János Horváth always asked me very friendly questions. But that is not the point, the point is that he not only had a profound understanding of Hungarian history, he not only had a deep Hungarian sensibility, but he also had a very good knowledge and perception of the world, as his famous letter to Zbigniew Brzeziński testifies. He had an excellent grasp of the essence of Visegrád cooperation, of Central Europe, of Central European identity and history. He knew the whole world and was open to it. He was the person in whom profound Hungarian self-identity and openness to the world, understanding and seeing it, were united in an exemplary way. Indeed, we could all learn from him. Have we learned enough? I am not sure. But let us not give up, because his memory is with us! And the very fact that so many of us are gathered here today shows that we are preserving his memory. Let us hold up his legacy, heed his spiritual messages, and follow his uprightness. I only wish that in this twenty-first century we will continue to have great Hungarians like János Horváth, who will shape the destiny of this country and this nation in the best possible direction.

Thank you very much.

Otto von Habsburg: His Life and Legacy

Delivered at the opening of the exhibition "The Life and Legacy of Otto von Habsburg" *at the Royal Palace in Gödöllő, 24 January 2020*[1]

Ladies and Gentlemen,

With great respect and love, I welcome everyone, especially family members. For once, I am not referring to members of my own big family, but to you, George and Charles. All the more so because, George, I know from you, as we have just heard, that Otto von Habsburg spent his last night before fleeing here in this palace. It is also from you that I know that when he returned to Hungary, his very first outing brought him here.

It is perhaps no coincidence, no, it is certainly not a coincidence, that when we were preparing for the Hungarian Presidency of Council of the European Union and had to decide on the venue for high-level events, we decided, at some risk, but of course with complete confidence in the efficiency of Mayor György Gémesi, that this palace should be that site. Not because I would come off exceptionally well by having to travel less, but because we felt and knew that the message of European unity could best be conveyed here, in this palace, which is closely related to the building of a united Europe as it is in-

---

[1] Published on the website of the Otto von Habsburg Foundation in 2020. https://habsburgottoalapitvany.hu

separable from the Habsburg family. This was therefore one of the important messages when choosing this palace.

I mentioned that it was not a coincidence, but, of course, there are many coincidences. "What seems an accident / in retrospect is fate." This is a quote from a poem by Roger Scruton, who, by the way, is to be buried today. In retrospect, everything looks like fate, the fate of a man, the fate of a family, the fate of a country, the fate of a nation, and, of course, the fate of Europe. You could say that history is a series of coincidences, but, of course, in retrospect, it is fate.

The question often arises what would have happened had historical events not taken place as they did. I do not consider this question to be superfluous at all. In fact, it is a very important and legitimate question. Incidentally, Géza Jeszenszky published a very fine essay on this not so long ago, and, if I may refer to myself, I also spoke about it at a conference a few weeks ago. Things could have happened differently as a matter of course. This is important because it means that we can shape not only the present but the future as well, for things can happen differently, and this is fundamentally up to us. In the case of the Habsburg family, we could go all the way back to the Middle Ages, but I should perhaps leave that to the historians here who are far more qualified than I am. But some questions can perhaps be raised from the more recent past.

What would have happened if the mission of Prince Sixtus had succeeded in 1916? Would King Charles and Queen Zita have managed to avoid the First World War? We do not know what would have happened, but we do know that the history of this country, Central Europe, and Europe would have been different. What would have happened if the Entente Powers had had the geopolitical vision and wisdom to understand that Europe did need a larger, stronger political union in Central Europe? What would have happened if the dream of the now forgotten Elemér Hantos, the *Mitteleuropäischer Postverein,* had been realized? It was not. What would have happened if Chancellor Schuschnigg had accepted Otto von Habsburg's proposal to abdicate his throne but assume the chancellorship of the Republic of Austria? That is not what happened. What would have happened—we could go on—if as a result there had been no Anschluss, and Hungary had not been a direct neighbour of Hitler's empire? And what would have happened if Otto von Habsburg had not taken on the patronage of the Pan-European Picnic, and as a consequence, perhaps the Pan-European Picnic and the breakthrough to Europe, the *Durchbruch*, had not taken place? And what would have happened if, under the influence of various factors, including the will of Otto von Habsburg, the circumstances of the regime-change turned out finally to have made Otto von Habsburg president of the Republic of Hungary? Perhaps he would have been better suited than the man who actually held that office to express and bring about national unity across party lines in the midst of a taxi blockade and a war over the media. But we will never know.

More interesting is whether we can foresee the future. We live in a world of economic and geopolitical forecasting, but we fail to foresee the future. And, yet, more and more of us know and see what is going to happen in the world. If we understood half as much about the present, we would be in a much better position. We come face to face with our inability to have foreseen or to foresee the future when we ask ourselves: Who on earth foresaw that in the late 1980s, the last years of communism, the most popular Hungarian would be called Otto von Habsburg? Who would have thought that Hungary would be represented in the European Parliament years before its membership of the European Union?

When we look at the photograph, which we will see here at the exhibition, of a four-year-old boy all dressed up in 1916 attire at the coronation of King Charles, we wonder what this little boy might have been thinking. Did he know what would happen to him? Certainly not. It is very interesting to read a report from the Hungarian ambassador to Madrid in the early 1920s, Iván Praznovszky. He said that the Spanish queen, Maria Christina, was delighted to have this particular ten-year-old boy at her home and was always happy to talk to this clever, kind, bright boy about Hungary. She showed him pictures of Hungary saying, "Believe me, my child, the Hungarian hussars are the best soldiers in the world, and you should be very proud of being a Hungarian." We owe gratitude to the queen because she was impeccably successful, for it was also owing to her that this little boy became a true Hungarian patriot, a Hungarian and a European giant in the history of the past decades. Both Hungarian and European, the two together. His whole life was an example of how this is possible.

As to personal memories—a good forty years ago, I was witness to a telephone conversation during which a great friend of mine, the late György O'sváth, repeatedly said "your majesty." I then, of course, asked him whom he was talking to, and that is when I learned the difference between the word "majesty" and "highness."[2] He addressed Otto von Habsburg as "your majesty." He did not call him "Your Honour" for his parliamentary membership or by his first name; he called him "Your Majesty" because he thought that was right and proper.

Otto von Habsburg was keen to know about all important aspects of the process of regime-change, including, for example, the details of the privatization process. I will never forget the very educational discussion we had about the electoral system. He explained—God forbid my giving this any political slant—that he believed truly democratic elections take place in individual constituencies. It is no coincidence that the British chose that, not wanting to vote for an obscure party on a closed party list, but for someone they more or less knew. But these are minor issues. In the end, I think we all learned a great deal from him.

I said a moment ago that history is a series of coincidences. Yes, but there is something inevitable about them. There is a law, the law implies regularity, and regularity implies necessity. Otto von Habsburg's entire life exemplifies the fact that it is necessary and inevitable that we are here, that Hungary exists. There is a Hungarian nation, there is a Hungarian nation in Europe. That we are both Hungarians and Europeans. He succeeded in this. I believe that he has set an example for us all. And yes, here we are. It is inevitable, it is necessary. We are all here: descendants of pro-Habsburg and anti-Habsburg Hungarians. Here we are, Leftist and Rightist. Here we are, believers and unbelievers. Here we are, liberals and conservatives. I will not go on, because names, denominations change, evolve, new ones always cropping up. We always have to find newer and newer designations for newer and newer groups, and that is as it should be.

Irrespective of that, we are here. We are and will be together. I am not using the word survival, because there is more to it than that. It was enabled by many in the history of Hungary, Central Europe, and Europe. It is a subject of debate whether the crowd or the individual personality has a greater role in history. However, we need not decide the debate, because we have had personalities—Otto von Habsburg above all—to shape our history. They have played a decisive role in the whole process of European integration and the

---

2   In Hungarian there is but a single consonant of difference between the words *felség* and *fenség*.

reunification of Europe, the incorporation of Central Europe, including Hungary, into the process of European unification.

In recalling my personal memories, I did not yet mention but will never forget the concrete professional, intellectual, political, and human support that Otto von Habsburg gave our country and nation in this process. This is why I am particularly grateful to you all, Gergely, and why I consider it a very special honour and pleasure to have been asked to give this short commemorative speech. Thank you very much for your attention.

Otto von Habsburg and Our Visions of Europe

Delivered at a conference of the Otto von Habsburg Foundation, 20 November 2020.

Welcome to virtual Hungary! I hope next time we will be able to continue our discussions in a face-to-face format. However, this is the age of digitalization—we might as well take advantage of it.

I learned a great deal from Minister Lamassoure's lecture. We have met and discussed Europe several times, and I am pleased to note once again that on the most important points we are always essentially in agreement.

It was eleven months ago that we had a conference on the life and legacy of Otto von Habsburg at Gödöllő Palace, close to my home. I made a short speech there, and, of course, we all stressed that Otto von Habsburg had been a great European who played a prominent, even determining role in the history of the building of Europe. I also said that he had been as a great Hungarian, a great patriot of Hungary, and—as her excellency the Spanish Ambassador has honoured us with her presence—I would like to repeat what I said at our last conference: I wish to express once again our gratitude to Her Royal Highness Maria Christina, the Queen of Spain at the time, who taught little Otto, and put it to him several times: "My dear child, you must be proud of being Hungarian, and you must also know that the Hungarian hussars are the best soldiers in the world." So, we owe our gratitude to Her Royal Highness Maria Christina because Otto turned out to be a proud Hungarian and a proud European at the same time, the perfect demonstration that you can have both a national and a European identity at once.

A few days ago, as I was wondering what today's topic would be, I asked our director Gergely [Pröhle]: "Are we going to talk about the life and legacy of Otto von Habsburg or about the future of Europe?" He failed to give a clear-cut answer, just telling me to talk about whatever I wanted to. Finally, I figured out a fair and simple answer: if we were going to talk about the legacy of Otto von Habsburg, we would inevitably talk about the future of Europe. And should we want to talk about the future of Europe, we must first trace the roots of this extraordinary seventy-year building project in the past. We must thus rediscover its origins and foundations, which would not be possible without evoking the great personalities that worked on this unparalleled edifice. Robert Schuman, Jean Monnet, and also, of course, Otto von Habsburg each had an enormous impact on this building venture. And it is an undertaking—fully concurring with Alain Lamassoure—that has been characterized by vast successes without precedent in the history of Europe.

Monsieur Lamassoure mentioned the institutions, and, again, I think we essentially concur on the matter, because despite all the difficulties and challenges, problems and misunderstandings, the institutions work. We have modified them several times, and today there are people who are perhaps trying to find solutions through the modification of the institutional set-up. On this point, I myself would be much more cautious, because if we tip this balance—there are efforts being made to that end—we might risk creating new problems instead of solving the existing ones.

Another area in which we have undoubtedly succeeded is the economy, starting with the Common Market, then the single market, and now even the single currency—for all its well-known difficulties and risks. We also have a formidable competition policy, and we have a largely successful cohesion policy. So, on the whole, we are justified in saying that the area of the economy is where integration has been most successful. But, of course, there are various other issues, dilemmas, challenges, and problems. I doubt I am tasked to list them all this evening. Yet I do wish to mention one or two. Firstly, there is a marked imbalance among the different areas of integration. One of the fundamental challenges is the imbalance between the economic and the political dimension. The economic dimension is—as we have said—an area of great success, for all the difficulties. The political dimension is a sort of half success, an area where we have conspicuous weaknesses. So, it is absolutely necessary to strengthen the political dimension—first and foremost, foreign and security policy, including common defence.

Alain Lamassoure dwelt on this dimension, as well. I think we all agree that we must move ahead on that front, otherwise the imbalance between the economic and the political dimensions will become even more problematic than it is today.

But there is another imbalance that is perhaps even more important—the lack of a balance between the economic-political dimension on the one hand and the cultural dimension on the other. It is in the cultural dimension that we really have a lot to do. I am not saying that we have neglected the cultural dimension; I am simply pointing out that it is a dimension where we lag behind, and that it is the source of our difficulties. These arise from the fact that the cultural dimension—put plainly, European identity—is not sufficiently developed. There are several reasons for this. First of all, there has always been a mistrust of community or collective identity in certain circles. The historical reasons for this aversion or suspicion are well known. But if we do not recognize collective identity, how are we going to accept and recognize national identity, which is not only the primary collective identity but also an indispensable cornerstone of any Europe-building? How can we recognize and define European identity? For European identity does exist, however we wrangle about the order and importance of its various constituent elements.

For some, it is the Christian or Judeo-Christian heritage that is most important. For some it is the ancient heritage, which is likewise indubitable. It is also generally recognized that the legal standards arising from the legacy of Roman law are not only the basis of Europe's legal culture but also an important element of European identity. We may emphasize different elements, but it is diversity that comprises the heart of European identity. We often refer to the principle of "unity in diversity," but we must admit that, in order for diversity to prevail, we need more flexibility and tolerance with regard to different approaches to or elements of European identity. If we really want to strengthen the cultural dimension of integration, we must first buttress European identity.

In all probability, culture is the foundation of all other areas. Technology has also been brought up. Europe is losing ground in the field of technology, as well as in that of demography. True enough. But do technology and demography not ultimately depend on culture? They all hinge on what is going on in our minds. So, we have to strengthen our individual and collective identities in order to underpin and improve our competitive position in the field of technology as well.

It is primarily for these reasons that we need to deal with the problem of the weakness, or even the absence, of European identity. We need to engage in dialogue, and, above all, we must listen to the other. We have to see that diversity is a reality because the historical, geographical, economic, and other circumstances are different in the various regions of Europe. Another difficulty often mentioned is the divisions between the Member States and the nations. These divisions are of various kinds, we need to discuss them, we need on-going dialogue about them. Once again, I would like to emphasize that we need tolerance in order to understand and accept the approach, conditions, and heritage of others. This is one of the main messages of Otto von Habsburg.

We have already talked and will talk about the serious crisis we are undergoing. There is a kind of uncertainty throughout the world, an individual and collective neurosis; there are tensions not only between small countries—several examples have been mentioned by Alain Lamassoure—but also big ones, the superpowers. Obviously, the tension is rising. Many are concerned about an armed conflict breaking out. I myself do not tend to think that is likely, but we must be on the alert, for we know from history that if a conflict dubbed a trade war escalates, the consequences can be tragic.

I see Europe's main role therein. The European Union should intervene with all the weight of its experience and culture, because we still do have an influence, even if technologically we are not the at top, and demographically we are in decline. But we still have—I am convinced—a kind of savoir-faire, a particular aptitude in the field of culture. We must not only keep but strengthen and wield it. It is by means of this special European cultural prowess that we should make a much greater contribution to the development of world affairs than hitherto and exert a greater influence on the future of the world.

This is Europe's true mission. We have succeeded in removing the threat of armed conflict between the great powers of Europe. We have discussed at length the unquestionably foundational Franco-German reconciliation, where again the role and the contribution of Otto von Habsburg must be underlined. But having overcome that risk, perhaps we have forgotten that there are other risks in the world, possible conflicts outside Europe in which we might intervene. These are not necessarily or not only economic or trade conflicts and tensions.

There are geopolitical conditions as well, and we need to have geopolitical weight, and to have geopolitical weight—importance and responsibility, as well—we need a much stronger foreign and defence policy, and a kind of synergy between the approaches of trade, economy, geopolitics, and security, because the links between them are ever closer.

In any case, it is obvious that we are the ones to solve our own problems. To this end, I think, we need to talk about substantial matters. We have modified, even improved the exceptional system several times—it was right and proper for us to do so. But if we only seek the means of continuing the integration process, or only focus on institutional reform, we will fail. The institutional reforms have been important and useful, but we have had our fill. We now need to talk about the essence: the values, the vision, the future, and we have to strengthen the kind of affiliation with, or attachment to Europe that we call identity.

So, again, I think that the example of the great persons who created Europe, to whom we owe this success story, must be followed. Robert Schuman spoke of an area of civilization, a spiritual and cultural community, Helmut Kohl of a *Wertegemeinschaft*, and Otto von Habsburg likewise stressed these. They were all fully aware of the fact that culture is essential to, is indeed the basis of this whole enterprise, and it is this area of civilization that we must defend.

We have thereby broached the fundamental question: that of security! External and internal security, border security. The security of the sovereign state. Now we are in the midst of a pandemic, which is a severe warning that security is paramount. It is in the midst of crises that we understand better that security is more important than any other dimension. And today, here we are, unfortunately, in the middle of a crisis which has brought it home to us why collective security must have absolute priority in certain situations. I hope that we can continue this dialogue, and that conferences like this, even in this virtual way, will contribute to the building and operation of this huge edifice we call European integration.

Difference or Gap?

Allow me to continue where Alain Lamassoure wound up. There is no gap. There are differences, divisions of various kinds, which are understandable. There is a North–South division, the causes of which are mainly economic and financial. There is also a West–East division, for essentially historical and cultural reasons. One of the aspects of this division was very clearly indicated by Alain Lamassoure, the kind of difference between the more communitarian approach in Central and Eastern Europe and the more individual one in Western Europe. In Lithuania, for example, there are several communities, as there are in other Central European countries, but they are all indigenous, not the results of migration. This is a major difference, because these communities, like the Hungarian national minority in neighbouring countries, want to preserve their cultural or national identities—their Hungarian identity, because they are Hungarian. They are not migrants. They have been here for a thousand years or more. This is a fundamental difference.

Another difference between the two regions—and also an explanation for this difference in approach to community or collective identity—is that, for a Pole or a Hungarian, national identity has always been an existential matter. If Hungarians lose their national identity, they cease to exist as a nation. The same applies to the religious heritage. Without Christianity, Poland or Hungary would not exist. Poland as a sovereign nation-state ceased to exist for a hundred and fifty years. It was the Catholic religion that that saved it. Christianity was more or less the same for Hungary. For one hundred and fifty years, the Ottoman Empire occupied the larger part of our national territory—a long period of struggle for the survival of the nation. We were therefore obliged to preserve our language, culture, heritage, and also our religion, not only individually but also and above all as a community. A community with a historical, cultural, and spiritual nature thus became, and still is, the indispensable framework of existence for us.

No, this is in no way an abyss; it is only an original difference in the historical heritages of these national communities. We must see and understand this difference, and we must also tolerate all possible divergences that have their roots in the historical, geographical, or even cultural particularities of the regions of Europe. We fully accept the great ideas of the Enlightenment—freedom, fraternity, and equality. We respect *laïcité,* because we understand the historical reasons why this principle is so important for our French friends.

Part I

I accept all this, as I accept other elements of European identity. My only wish is that our approaches and priorities be likewise accepted. For example, the Christian heritage could and should have been included in the draft constitutional treaty. It was not—we know the story full well. But it would have been an important message of tolerance and, at the same time, the recognition of the reality that the Christian heritage is essential for the existence and the future of Europe. We therefore need a debate, an open and sincere discussion, which is precisely what we are doing here. Let me repeat, our approaches are almost identical with those of Alain Lamassoure, in any case they are very close. It is proof that there is common ground between the different approaches. We need these debates, we need to continue such dialogue, with a view to extending this common ground as far as possible.

Thank you for your attention!

A "Temporary Paradise" on the Road to Freedom

This speech was delivered, in French, at the Les soldats français réfugiés en Hongrie 1940–1945 *(French Refugees in Hungary) conference at the Institut Français de Budapest, 10 October 2018.*[1]

At the high school in Balatonboglár twenty-six years ago, there was a group of more than twenty people, ladies and gentlemen in their seventies among them. All were elegantly dressed, their faces expressive–sometimes smiling, but often with tears in their eyes...

These ladies and gentlemen—some of them still speaking fairly good Hungarian—had all been participants, actors, and even protagonists in a miracle. What is a miracle? It is a pure, simple story, very easy to understand for those who want to. Because it expresses a profound truth, the essential meaning of our human condition. It also expresses fundamental human values such as brotherhood, solidarity, freedom, and all the basic elements of what we call today European identity.

At this solemn occasion commemorating the "temporary paradise" French prisoners of war who escaped during the Second World War found in Hungary, I was among the speakers, a young secretary of state, representing my government. The meeting with the escaped POWs and their wives filled me with enormous strength, energy, and optimism. Optimism for the future of

---

[1] It was published on the website of the Hungarian Embassy in Paris in 2018.

my country, the future of Europe, and also for the future of relations between France and Hungary.

That is how it was in the early 1990s, after the regime-change, also called a constitutional revolution. We were full of hope, ambition, and determination, full of confidence in ourselves. A fundamental transformation was underway both internally and externally. The old international structures, such as the Warsaw Pact and Comecon, had already been dismantled, and we had begun to build new relationships. Negotiations on the association agreement with the European Community were in progress, and we had declared our intention to join the European Community and NATO.

One of the pillars of our foreign policy was to establish balanced and friendly relations with all Western European countries. Within the framework of this policy, I myself repeatedly stressed the need to strengthen French presence—economic, political, and cultural presence—in Hungary, regardless of the difficulties, bitterness, and grievances of the past. And yes, we can say that we have made progress, we have even achieved important results not only on the economic level but also in the fields of political and especially cultural relations, including our respective knowledge and understanding of the other. We have developed mutual empathy–and all this within a common framework, European integration. It can therefore be said with confidence that today Franco–Hungarian relations are deeper and stronger than they were twenty-six years ago.

And here we are, together, facing common tasks and the enormous challenge of how to continue building Europe, how to find, to recover the soul of Europe. We must therefore reflect on, think and speak about, discuss, and understand Europe. First of all, we have to find the collective identity of Europe, that is to say, to rediscover and strengthen the cultural dimension, which is the basis of all the processes of economic and political integration. One has to accept oneself, also in a collective way, and to do so, the essential and common elements need to be found in an impartial, balanced, tolerant, and respectful way, without prejudice and hypocrisy. There may be differences in priorities, there may be different approaches stemming from historical heritage and experience, but what is important is to find the essentials and to simultaneously recognize, respect, and accept the divergences of tone that exist between us. Essentially, the soul of Europe is that we discover the values that are common to us; these bind us together and unite us in our shared aspirations.

This is the message to us of the miracle of the escaped French POWs and their temporary paradise in Hungary—an episode that has made history.

Speech Commemorating the Revolution and War of Independence in 1848-1849

Delivered at the commemoration ceremony in Erzsébet Park, Sepsiszentgyörgy (Sfântu Gheorghe, Romania) on 15 March 2019.

You spoke right from my heart, Mr Mayor![1] Indeed, you have touched upon much of what I intended to say. But it is all right; some things cannot be repeated often enough.

Dear friends, dear celebrators,

First of all, a word of thanks. Thank you for the amazing and incredible experience that I am having here today as we celebrate the feast of our Hungarianness and freedom together. Perhaps I must thank the Good Lord above that I am celebrating this national holiday in the heart of Székely Land for the first time in my life; perhaps a little late, yet I did come to be with Székely Hungarians on this day. I am grateful to the Good Lord but also to you for keeping alive the spark of Hungarian identity and liberty here in Székely Land and Transylvania for 171 years, even under difficult circumstances. Thanks be to you! We Hungarians of the mother country owe you great gratitude for this. I am not sure we have always guarded this spark in the same way at home. But let me also ask, ask the Almighty to let Székely Hungarians celebrate this holiday in the same way in the coming decades, centuries, for as long as the world lasts, as long as people live on Earth. All we Hungarians ask the Good God to help us in this.

---

[1] András Árpád Antal, Mayor of Sepsiszentgyörgy (Sfântu Gheorghe, Romania)

Speech Commemorating the Revolution and War of Independence in 1848–1849

What is a national holiday? A national holiday always offers a dense message; a concise expression of what our past has to say to us, to the present and to the future. It gives us a sense of life and a vision of the world. It is no mere coincidence that we say that this holiday is a celebration of Hungarian identity and freedom, because there is something very special, very peculiarly Hungarian about it.

I have been considering these few questions for a long time. Why is it that, throughout their history and far beyond their strength and numbers, Hungarians have contributed to the realization of the ideal of freedom in the world? Why is it that all of our fights for freedom have at first been crushed, but then, a few decades later, have achieved victory? Why is it that when we celebrate our national holidays, when we celebrate freedom, we always remember our martyrs? We must always think first of those who gave their lives for our homeland and our freedom. This is the way we are, and this is why we say, as the mayor has just said, that the essence of our soul, the heart of our identity is freedom. Without it, we would not be Hungarians. So it was after 15 March 1848, and so it was on 23 October 1956. It was upon the latter date that Sándor Márai wrote:

> More and more ask it, there seems no end,
> Haltingly, for they can't comprehend –
> Those, for whom Freedom bequest had brought,
> Ask it: is Freedom so great a thought?[2]

Yes, freedom is so a great a thought! And surely you have all noticed that in the Hungarian language, in Hungarian literature, poetry, and history, we do not have separate words for individual freedom and the freedom of the community—national independence, as we might otherwise term it. One word expresses it all. Another interesting thing about freedom is that it is—to use a current term—not a zero-sum game. Because the more freedom I have, the more freedom all others have. Freedom is not exclusive. Freedom is for everyone. Like love. The more love I have, the more I will be loved. It is no coincidence that it occurred to a Hungarian poet to link freedom and love.

---

2   Sándor Márai, "Angel from heaven", translated by Leslie A. Kery.

Part I

Everyone knows its few lines; I shall not read them out.[3] Hundreds of millions of Chinese children learn the poem in their curriculum and can recite it. In Chinese, of course.

But, if it is true that individual freedom and community freedom cannot be separated, it must also be true that individual rights cannot be separated from the rights of communities, without which there is no individual freedom. And there are no true community rights without individual rights. And community rights mean that the community has the right to manage its own affairs. It determines its ways, governs itself, and administers itself. This is called self-rule, self-determination, self-administration, most usually, autonomy. What is autonomy? First of all, autonomy is in our souls, in our hearts, within us. We are autonomous, we decide our own affairs, and we want to decide the affairs of our own community. What does a community insist on? It insists on its past and its traditions, its heritage, and, of course, its present and its future.

What is a community entitled to do? It has a right to its language, its values, its identity, its symbols, its insignia and flag, its region, because autonomy is increasingly regional. That is why what you have achieved is a great success: the decision of the European Court of Justice, which lays down the basis for recognizing cultural-national identity. A lot of work still has to be done to fully establish it, but the process has started. We are grateful for that, and we celebrate those who were instrumental in the achievement.

Dear Friends! My life and the lives of many of us have been about two things. One is the strengthening of Hungarians' sense of belonging together, especially with regard to improving the real situation and the legal status of cross-border Hungarian communities. The other is the ever-stronger involvement of all Hungarians in European processes, in the process of European integration. We believed that the two are interlinked, and the more success we achieved in the second area, the more results we would achieve in the first. This did not fully come true. But it must be seen that if Europe wants to over-

---

3 Freedom and love my creed!
  These are the two I need.
  For love I'll freely sacrifice
  My earthly spell,
  For freedom, I will sacrifice
  My love as well.

come its current difficulties and challenges, it will inevitably have to take into account, accept, recognize, and acknowledge the existence of national communities, national minorities, nationalities, and, above all, national regions. This is what a truly successful Europe can be one day.

And, of course, having as many Hungarians as possible hold seats in the European Parliament in the future will make an important difference. The twenty-one seats Hungary has cannot be increased. We might be able to increase those numbers for others, but this depends on you. We can only assist you. We Hungarians and Székelys are but a handful. But we must also know that great things depend not on size, on numbers, but on will, resolve, and spirit. Great things depend on inner strength, the purity of value choices, free will, and the will to be free.

May God bless all the Hungarian and Székely people.

Thank you very much.

Hungarian Diplomacy Day

Delivered at an event organized by the Faculty of Public Governance and International Studies at the University of Public Service in Budapest, 21 November 2019.[1]

Dear colleagues, dear students,

Hungarian Diplomacy Day is first and foremost a day of remembrance and acknowledgement, expressing thanks to all those who represent the interests of our country in any area of international relations and who further them to the best of their ability. But who are diplomats? In the broadest sense, everyone, all of us. All those who, in their respective positions, serve the interests of this nation and work to enhance the reputation of our country. The circle of diplomats cannot therefore be reduced to ambassadors and other professional diplomats because we all have a duty to serve our country.

What is diplomacy really? According to the recently published *Dictionary of Diplomacy*,[2] a rather complicated definition of the term is that it means both an organization and the activities of that organization. But there is a simpler definition. Diplomacy is nothing other than a relationship with the world, a relationship with different states, organizations, and, above all,

---

[1] Published in Hungarian in *Magyar Szemle*, volume XXIX, 2020, numbers 7–8, 118–120.
[2] Bába, Iván and János Sáringer (eds.), *Diplomáciai Lexikon - A nemzetközi kapcsolatok kézikönyve*, Budapest: Éghajlat, 2018, 722.

with people. Its main objective is peace, security, and trust in and friendship with the world, always and above all in the interests of the Hungarian state and nation.

It is no coincidence that Hungarian Diplomacy Day falls on the day of the Czech, Polish, and Hungarian kings' meeting in Visegrád in 1335. The most important message in this is that the primary aim of foreign policy is to strengthen relations with our neighbours, because it is always the neighbour whom we must rely on in times of trouble, and it is with our neighbours that we must first and foremost live in friendship and trust. This is true even if we have not been able to live up to it throughout our histories. But the very purpose of diplomacy is to defuse and resolve possible tensions and to promote prosperity and cooperation in the region that serves as our home.

This why we chose this day, which both refers back to the historical foundation of the current Visegrád cooperation and also marks the fact that Central European cooperation is not only the most successful but also the most important area of Hungarian foreign policy.

We are back in Europe and are back to stay. As we say, Europe is our home, Hungary is our homeland. We are part of the Western world, and we embrace its values while we are open to the whole world. Above all, we preserve our national identity, but we combine it with our Central European and European identity. We believe in the values of the European way of life and in the need to preserve and defend these values. We believe in the dignity, freedom, equality, and responsibility of human beings, as Christian theology discovered a thousand years ago. We believe in equality, freedom and fraternity, and that European civilisation must embrace and assert all these values, today and in the future. It is our belonging to the European and Western world that enables us to open up to the rest of the world. We must never forget that bridges can only be built between bridgeheads, and we are not a bridge but a bridgehead. A good example of our openness to the world is the Stipendium Hungaricum scholarship scheme, which enables so many young people to understand, appreciate, and love Hungary.

What then is Europe, where are its borders, where do we place the civilizational boundary between Europe and Asia? There is no doubt that there are many similarities between them, but there are also significant differences. The place of Hungarians is in Europe, and this is despite the fact that we come from the East.

Part I

The task of a Hungarian diplomat is particularly difficult and complex. She or he must not simply represent a particular state, Hungary, but the Hungarian nation as a whole. As history has shown, in our case the borders of nation and of state do not coincide, and we must never forget that as Hungarians we have a duty that no Hungarian government, no Hungarian political party, no Hungarian diplomat, and no Hungarian person can forget: the interests of the Hungarian state and the Hungarian nation must never come into conflict with each other, and we must represent the interests of the entire Hungarian national community. Our national identity, our sense of belonging to the nation, leads to Europeanness, and Europeanness leads to the universal community, which we can express most pithily with our Hungarian word for humanity, *emberiség*.

Dear students, I am sure many of you are considering a career in diplomacy. I hope you will realize this goal. Acquire strong theoretical foundations and develop your practical skills, because this is how you will be able contribute to the success of Hungary, the Hungarian nation, our region, and Europe as a whole. In this way we will live in peace, security, and friendship not only with our neighbours but with the whole world.

I wish you every success in your deliberations today.

Speech Commemorating Heroes' Day

Delivered at Szada on Heroes' Day, 7 June 2020.

Dear Mr. Mayor, representatives of Church Communities, citizens of Szada, and dear friends,

Every year we commemorate the heroes of Szada. The very first thought that comes to mind is one of gratefulness—we say thanks to the Chief Executive for the weather, for we have come together even though we had originally thought we would have to make do with broadcasting this event by local television, without being physically together on the very day of National Unity or the day after. I am thankful for that, because, if I do not see the eyes, the young, and the not so young in front of me as I speak, I find it difficult to say anything.

I wanted to address those present as Honourable Commemorators and Celebrators! How can these two things go together? Because we are commemorating a tragedy, we are commemorating the Hungarian heroes of Szada, but we are also celebrating something.

But, perhaps first, a word about the tragedy is due. We all know that the greatest tragedy of this nation, of our thousand-year history, is the Trianon Peace Dictate. The facts are known, they have been referred to here, I will not repeat them. The loss of territory, the loss of one third of the people belonging to the Hungarian nation, their separation from us by the borders—these are facts that can be measured, expressed in figures. But what is really impor-

Part I

tant cannot be thus expressed, for it is in our souls and in our hearts. The loss, the pain will never go away. This is the tragedy. It is also said that perhaps never before in history has a country been carved up and divided like we were. Albert Apponyi has just been referred to. He said that our grave was dug; but, my dear friends, our grave was indeed dug, but we failed to lie in it.

"Not perished as asked—can't comprehend. / Why not in silence await the end?" as Sándor Márai put it.[1] Well, we did not perish, did not in silence await the end. Even though in the hundred years that followed the tragedy we suffered so many heavy blows, so many losses, and so many Hungarian heroes, so many heroes of Szada sacrificed themselves for the homeland, for the nation.

So, how come we celebrate? We celebrate because this greatest tragedy, turned into a miracle, a Hungarian miracle, the miracle of a hundred years. We cannot explain it, we cannot really tell it. But we can preserve it because it is our miracle. The miracle of survival, of endurance, of empowerment, and of spiritual and intellectual strength. And, for all the many tragedies that followed, the miracle of economic, institutional, and political consolidation.

A few words must be said about whom we owe gratitude to. First and foremost, I believe we owe our thanks to all Hungarians, all Hungarians without exception, yet especially to cross-border Hungarians. Had they not persevered, not stood by us, this miracle would never have happened. Thanks be therefore to all the Hungarians of the world, wherever they are, for their perseverance and support. Thanks be also to the Hungarians of the motherland. We also owe thanks to the churches, which played a decisive role in the endurance of the Hungarian language, culture, spirit, thinking, soul, and faith. We owe thanks to the heroes we cannot list. We owe our thanks to the likes of Miklós Bánffy, who returned to Transylvania to work and suffer for it and the nation. To the likes of Kuno Klebelsberg, who immediately understood that it was alright not to be allowed to build a strong army; we could instead build public schools in every village in Hungary. Hungarian children would then learn; and, thus, universities and clinics were built for those that had learned. Well, that, my dear friends, was the real miracle. Perhaps the current period also has had its achievements because, first, we were able to recognize

---

1 "Angel from Heaven", translated by Leslie A. Kery.

the membership of cross-border Hungarians in the nation, and second, we were able award Hungarian state citizenship to them.

Every Hungarian is responsible for every Hungarian, said the writer Dezső Szabó. This is a great truth. But if we take a broader view, we can also say that every person is responsible for every person. This is the idea of humankind, which emerges very well in the Hungarian word *emberiség* ("humanity"). But then where do we begin? Where those who are closest to us are: with the family. Because without healthy families there is no healthy society, no healthy nation. And then we continue with the communities close to us. With our own village, with Szada! Above all, we should remember our own heroes. For they are our heroes, both those who had lived here for generations and those who came later. That was how we become a community, we share heroes, we share lives, and we depend on each other. We owe our gratitude to those that safeguarded this essence of Szada, and to those Székelys of Szada, who came here, integrated with and enriched the community.

And then, of course, we continue with wider groups, cities, churches, other communities, and the most important community, the nation. Beginning with the family, the village, the larger communities, we continue with the nation—and that is also how the memory of tragedy is condensed into one big, shared pain. And we all feel that pain. Indeed, there is hardly any Hungarian who has not suffered a direct or indirect loss because of the Trianon Peace Dictate. It is our common experience, and that is why we commemorate it together, and why we share our celebration.

Our celebration of the miracle! We know that bells rang in many thousands of churches around the world at half past four on 4 June, the 100th anniversary of the Treaty of Trianon. All over the world. Eight Hungarian churches in Cleveland alone rang their bells; bells tolled from Australia to Austria, from Argentina to Canada. But perhaps the most important thing is not that these bells were rung but that they tolled in us, in our hearts. Anyone who has read Sándor Csoóri's poem "Bells Peal in Me" will have a sense of what this means. True bells peal in us. External chimes help, but it is the feeling, the spirit, that tolls in us.

Dear Friends, Szada citizens, and Hungarians, I only ask and wish that this peal remain in us for as long as Hungarians live on Earth, that this bell will always toll in us, that we never forget the tragedy, never forget the miracle. Let us save the memory of the tragedy, the memory of our heroes, but let

Part I

us cherish and save the miracle, the experience of the miracle, let us pass it on to future generations. And, as long Hungarians live on Earth, we will always celebrate the miracle.

Thank you very much for your attention!

Part II

World Trade in the Grip of Geopolitics

Investor-state Dispute Settlement and the Autonomy of EU Law: A Battle of Tribunals?

Speech to the HCCI / Hungarian Ministry of Justice Conference: Hungarian Arbitration on UNCITRAL Bases, 14 November 2018[1]

The settlement of investment disputes has become not only one of the most important legal issues in the field of the promotion, protection, and regulation of foreign investments but is now the focus of a much wider debate involving fundamental political, indeed ideological issues. One might say it is now the preferred battlefield of opponents and proponents of globalisation, whatever the syndrome of globalization means for the parties to this debate. Investor-State Dispute Settlement (ISDS) is a reflection of the „clash of ideologies."

The question that legal scholarship and practice now have to answer is how this battle can be moderated. How can the generally recognised serious flaws and deficiencies of both a procedural nature (lack of transparency, lack of consistency, issue-conflicts, costs, absence of review, etc.) and of substance (undue privileges for foreign investors, discrimination against domestic ones etc) of the existing dispute settlement system be eliminated? How can the international legal framework for ISDS be improved or renewed? And how can the conflicting interests of investors, host states, and all other stakeholders be rebalanced and attuned in an adjusted, reformed or renewed system that would also contribute to the strengthening of the international legal framework?

---

[1] Published in HVG Oracle, 2019, 428–430.

Considering the divergent, in fact, opposing views it seems that the option of taking no action is not a viable one, as it would jeopardize the achievement of the original and underlying purpose of the settlement of investment disputes and thereby foreign investments themselves. This is the reason why the United Nations Commission on International Trade Law (UNCITRAL) decided to establish a working group to identify issues, consider reform, and possibly develop relevant solutions. The language is extremely cautious, but the need is urgent. One can only hope that the debate will be depoliticized as much as possible (UNCITRAL has the best chances for that), and a more balanced and more efficient system enjoying wide support can ultimately be arrived at.

However, the work going on in the UNCITRAL will take a very long time, and the envisioned Multilateral Investment Court with its tenured judges, transparency and consistency, possibility of review, lower costs etc., is not to be put in place soon. In the meantime, the number of controversial issues continues to grow and creates special challenges to both theory and practice.

One of the challenges to the existing ISDS is the strengthening and expanding concept of the autonomy of EU law and more particularly the absence of a clear definition and precise scope of application of this concept based upon a well-established doctrine reflected in the case law of the CJEU.

The issue is also related to the much-disputed nature of European integration in general (international organisation v. quasi federal state) and consequently of the constitutional character and the autonomy of European law. One relevant aspect of this underlying dilemma is the relationship between international law and European law (the primary European law being itself international law).

The direct effect of international law in European law has never been fully and unconditionally recognized by the jurisprudence of the Court. Legal scholarship has pointed out that until 2008 the direct effect was a rebuttable presumption, and it was only denied in case the absence of certain conditions (clear, precise, unconditional rule) could be proven and the nature or the structure of the rule did not exclude the direct effect. (Right from the beginning an exception from this general rule has been in the GATT/WTO area; United Fruit, 21-24/72).

The most important turning points were the Kadi judgments, which first referred to the autonomy of EU law (Kadi I) and then clearly underlined that international law can only be applied (permeate the autonomous European legal order) if it is in line with the conditions as created by the basic principles of European law (Kadi II).

The principle of autonomy of European law is not limited to the area of human rights. One of the legal fields where the concept of the autonomy robustly appeared is the settlement of investment disputes, more particularly regarding the dispute settlement clauses of intra-EU bilateral investment protection treaties.

The problem with the much debated and criticised Achmea judgment is not that it declared that arbitration clauses of intra-EU BITs are incompatible with EU law and considered invalid. Scholarship and practice amply point out that the reasons given by the judgment are not sufficiently clear, give rise to conflicting interpretations, as some find them too broad (some even raise the question whether traditional rules of conflict of laws will be fully respected by a broad interpretation of the Achmea principle), and some are of the view that they are, indeed, too narrow. It is not clear what is the precise scope of the application of the Achmea arguments, to what extent Articles 267 and 344 of TFEU are relevant to other investment protection schemes, for instance the Energy Charter (ECT), and as a result where exactly the lines of the autonomy of EU law are to be drawn in future cases.

The situation ensuing from the shoreless wording of Achmea is at best confusing, at worst chaotic. International arbitrators reacted immediately. First, they rejected the applicability of the Achmea principle to the ECT (Masdar v. Spain, Vattenfall v. Germany) but also declined to follow the Achmea logic in an intra-EU BIT dispute (UP and CD Holding Int. v. Hungary), using the otherwise doubtful argument that ICSID cases are just different...

At the same time, the European Commission maintains its position that all intra-EU arbitration clauses are invalid and that this applies to multilateral instruments as well, where non-EU members (and the EU itself) are also parties (ECT).

However, the present situation, the ongoing battle of tribunals, will probably not hold for a long time. A regulation is now drafted by the European Commission providing for the immediate cancellation of all intra-EU BITs.[2]

---

[2] In the meantime, the concept changed and the idea of drafting and proposing a new regulation providing for the cancellation of all intra-EU BITs has been dropped. Instead of a new regulation,

Part II

Meanwhile the CJEU is expected to bring a judgment in the CETA case submitted by Belgium to the Court. For what that decision will be, guidance can be taken from Achmea itself, which refers to the possibility that the EU may create international courts in external relations, provided the autonomy of the EU and its legal order is respected. (What that precisely means and how this autonomy that some call a „catch all concept" will be interpreted, we will know when we have the next ruling of CJEU.) It should also be noted that the main proponent of the creation of a Multilateral Investment Court by a new international treaty to be elaborated by UNCITRAL is the European Union.

While the present legal uncertainty will likely be mitigated, no clear-cut, watertight outcome is to be expected.

Scholarship will have a brilliant subject to discuss, to write and to organize conferences about. Practice will participate in the debate, but in the meantime, it may take some practical measures, such as avoiding locating arbitration hearings in EU member countries and busily studying ways and means of the chances and possibilities to enforce arbitration awards outside the European Union.

---

an International Agreement is now being negotiated by the Member States for the Termination of (Bilateral) Investment Treaties between the Member States of the European Union. (The brackets around the word „bilateral" indicate the conflicting positions regarding the inclusion of the Energy Charter Treaty in the Agreement.) Prior to starting these negotiations, a Declaration was adopted by the Member States on 15 January 2019 on the legal consequences of the Achmea judgment and on investment protection. According to this Declaration all investor-State arbitration clauses contained in bilateral investment treaties concluded between Member States are contrary to Union law and thus inapplicable. Therefore, an arbitral tribunal established on the basis of investor-State arbitration clauses lacks jurisdiction. (Hungary made a separate declaration underlining that the future applicability of the Energy Charter Treaty in intra-EU relations requires further discussion and individual agreement amongst the Member States.)

The New World Order 2018
Integration and Multipolarity

Pallas Athéné Foundation for Innovation and Geopolitics, New World Order International Conference. 8 November 2018, Budapest.

First and foremost, I would like to congratulate Mr. Huang on his fascinating speech. I shall react to some of his ideas at a later stage. However, at the beginning I would like to take a more general approach. I also have to reveal that I got into politics by accident, as for decades I have been an international trade lawyer and have been teaching trade policy and law. Perhaps that is one of the reasons why I liked your presentation so much, Mr. Huang.

Starting with more general issues, my question is very simple. What do you think is the main driver of human history? Of course, there are different answers to this in different philosophical approaches. My answer is also very simple: the main driver of human history is culture. It is what is in our mind. To try to prove it very briefly: the two things that have the most sustained and strongest effect upon all geopolitical developments are demography and technology. Both demography and technology depend ultimately upon culture. To what extent do we want and are we willing to reproduce ourselves, individually and collectively? To what extent are we innovative and to what extent do we have the necessary degree of education and the capability to develop technology? All depends upon our mind. The second basic point of departure is that human nature is competitive. We are competing. It is deeply engrained in humankind that we compete individually and collectively. Collective competition is more interesting from the point of view of our subject this morning. Who are competing? We all know that civilizations, continents, political constitutional units are all competing—we call them states, sometimes we call them integration schemes. All these are constitutional units, but behind them there are a couple of factors such as territory, ideology. But—even if some people are a little bit hesitant to accept it—behind all these is what we call cultural heritage. We call it collective cultural identity. All this is part of the collective competition in which we are all involved.

The next question, before coming to the subject, is in what areas are we competing? We are competing practically everywhere. We are competing in trade, even if sometimes we are mistaken about the roots and the backgrounds. We are competing in economic performance, technology, technologic advancement and development. We are also competing in political power, in military capabilities, in military power. All that can be translated into an arms race. We are also competing in culture, in sports—fair or unfair; it is perhaps one of the most popular competitions of the world. To sum up, there are three main areas of competition. The first can be termed as trade, that is, in a more general sense, the economy. The second is the flag, that is the competition among political units, with all the increased risks involved. And the third is what we call in a symbolic sense the Bible or the Veda or the Koran—briefly, the Holy Scriptures representing ideas and visions. This third area is now often called ideology, although some of us feel some reluctance to use this word, for evident reasons.

The competition between ideas, visions, or ideologies has a direct and decisive effect upon the social, economic, and political model of the society we want to develop.

One problem that I see here is a recent development: all through human history these areas were relatively distinct from one another. For example, trade and security, which were always interdependent but were distinct, are now converging. There are many examples of that. For instance, when the United States introduced trade restrictions on steel imports, they referred to national security. National security in the system of the WTO always used to be a kind of exception; now it seems to be the main reference point. Of course, there is always an argument that if I do not have a prosperous steel industry, then my national security will be put in danger.

Now security and trade are converging; to some extent they are even considered to be identical. This is a serious issue, and it brings us back to the relationship between the flag and the trade. This is well reflected in the present relationship between the United States and China. Mr. Huang's presentation made it very clear that trade itself should not be a real problem. The answer to this is that indeed, it is not. In the old times, trade was a moderating factor. Conventional wisdom was that if you have very close trade relations then you have less reason to indulge in confrontation, possibly war, because the cost of war would be high due to the high degree of interdependence of the economies. Maybe yes, maybe no. World War I and II gave a different example. Do not forget that before World War II trade between Nazi Germany and the Soviet Union was extremely intensive, even in the final weeks, days, and hours.

For the time being, it seems trade is, in fact, not the real cause but rather it is the effect. Because the real reason behind the trade-war is geopolitical. It is security. It is how to slow down, how to stop the rise of China. It is not a secret. If you read the speech of Mike Pence of the 4th of October or if you just follow the speech of the president of the United States from the day before yesterday, it is quite clear that trade is a device for how the rise of China could be slowed down. Whether this is the right or the wrong way, I do not want to make judgements here, but clearly, there is now an overlapping between the trade and the flag, the latter representing security, geopolitical interest, and political power.

My original intention was to say some words about the structure of world power. We heard this morning and we hear everywhere that we now have a multipolar world. It was bipolar at the time of the cold war, and then perhaps for a very limited time it was unipolar. Then it became multipolar, although we do not know exactly where the poles are and what their position is relative to one another. Some people think—and this is linked to the G2, G7, and G0 theory—and Niall Ferguson says, that basically we are living in a G0 world, and that is something I can sympathize with. This means that maybe we are living not just in a multipolar but also to some extent in a nonpolar world.

Poles or no poles, I would call the world we are living in now a heterarchical world. Heterarchy is, in a way, the opposite of hierarchy. Heterarchy is an interesting structure of elements which was invented by neuroscientists based upon their research on the human brain. The human brain is a highly organized orderly structure, but it is not hierarchic. Similarly, the world geopolitical structure or order is not hierarchical. There are of course hierarchic, vertical structures, but at the same time, there are also horizontal connections. The world is not ranked but unranked or, more precisely, it may be ranked, but it is ranked in different ways. Just to give you some examples. On the top, we have the G2, China and the United States of America ranked on the basis of their economic performance, GDP, trade, military capabilities. These are the top two. Next come at least three very important players. The European Union, Russia, and Japan. In terms of military ranking Russia is essentially equal to the United States, especially and primarily in terms of the number of nuclear warheads. Only the two of them: Russia and the United States. China is lagging far behind them.

As regards economic performance, the European Union—at least for the time being with the United Kingdom—is in any case number one or two in terms of economic power, in terms of economic output, share in world trade and market size. However, at the same time where is the European Union in terms of military capabilities? Nowhere. Or political clouts? A little bit more but not too much, as we all know.

Japan is an important player, but they are not number one. They are not number one in economic output, in international trade, in military capacities, but they are very strong in all these areas. Moreover, geopolitically they are particularly important because they are very close to China geographically; at the same time, they are very close ideologically and in terms of the model of society to the United States.

The next layers you find in different spots on the map: for example, India. Because India demographically is as important as China—maybe more important even now or definitely in a couple of years. In terms of GDP, in terms of military capabilities India is lagging very much behind. We have other emerging powers, like Brazil and others. In the third layer, in about five months, we will have the next player, the newcomer. This newcomer is called the United Kingdom. If it remains united, as we hope it will, we will see the outcome. In any case, the United Kingdom will be a nuclear power—among the first five or six in the world—but in terms of economic output the rank is number five or six, soon seven or eight.

The structure is complex; it is heterarchic, but it is also volatile, it is changing. That creates the risks. Remember the so-called Thucydides trap, which means that rising powers always try to challenge the existing establishment. It is in a way normal. The structure that I try to describe is not just complex and complicated but, as I said, subject to permanent changes. There is a risk of rivalry, a risk of confrontation, a risk of overall animosity covering different areas —not just trade and technology but it also involves the flag as a constitutional unit, and that spells increased danger. That is why some people say that what we have now between the United States and China is not simply a trade war but something like a cold war. There is no definition for a cold war. We know from our memory what it looked like—the cold war before '89, '90—but we also see the differences. Because it is not exactly the same. However, there are elements that show that if it becomes an across-the-board, strategic rivalry or confrontation then it will get close to what we used to call cold war. We have —and that is a good sign—no wars by proxies. In the cold war there were lots of military conflicts by proxies. Now we have a few skirmishes here and there, but no proxy wars. At the same time, we have new, even more dangerous risks of war: we have cyber war, hybrid war, etc. So the world is becoming a riskier and more dangerous place, which needs particular attention and care.

My basic conclusion—one of them at least—is that I do not believe in dichotomy. I do not believe in that bipolar structure of the world. Whether it is trade, whether it is the economy, the flag, the geopolitical position, the "Bible," that is the culture, the world vision. We have several world visions; we have more than two models of society, we have several models of society. This kind of artificial division into black and white, white and black depending upon whose view it is, is to my mind wrong. The world is much more complex and much more complicated. This equally applies to all the three areas: trade, flag and Bible.

The second question I wanted to raise and perhaps try to answer regards the role of the second layer in this situation, which is the European Union, Russia, Japan, and perhaps India and others. How are they impacted or affected by this strategic rivalry emerging and getting stronger and deeper between the United States and China? How can they react to it? What is their interest? In terms of trade, some people say that Europe can be the "smiling third." That could be the case for a limited time, for some products; some limited marketshares could be captured here and there because of the trade restrictions introduced by both the United States and China. But on a more general level the "smiling third" approach is utterly wrong. The long term, negative impact of a real trade war between the United States and China will trump and far outweigh the possible small, temporary benefits that Europe might draw from this war. So, the next question is what Europe can do so that this trade war first, does not become a cold war and second, what it can do to moderate or mitigate the overall economic impact of this trade war. Here of course I think that the European Union does have a distinct role to play.

The European Union is not a by-stander, not even a mediator—because we do not want to mediate, we want to project messages. We want to project our visions. What are they? Rules. I am still one of those who believes in rules, first values, principles, and then rules. I still believe—whether this is obsolete or not—in multilateral rules and systems, provided we—more or less—all try to respect them and to comply with them. Now here we have the challenges. We have seen a very good film about the round table and the rectangular table. How can or could the Chinese round table be made more rectangular? We have some ideas. The European Commission prepared a paper about the reforms to be carried out with the WTO. So ideas are coming up now, primarily from Europe, because Europe learned how to reconcile different techniques, traditions, approaches and even different languages. So, the European way of rulemaking is a laboratory for a global approach, for global rule making for the creation of universal norms.

The argument is true that some are alien to this system because we expected more to happen from China at the time of the Chinese accession into WTO in 2001. The expectations have largely failed to materialize. Why? That is a different question. What will happen in the future, we do not know. I cannot be too optimistic, but you should never give up.

On the other hand, if there are difficulties in the functioning of a system, the solution is not to dismantle, deconstruct, and destroy the system. In such a situation, you have to save the system, and in order to save the system you have to reform the system. You have to and you can reform it. You have to tackle, for example, undue state influence via state-owned enterprises and heavy subsidies and the financial system and an allocation of national resources, which are ultimately under control of the party. You have to look into that. We also have some problems in other countries, so we cannot really reduce it to China. We have various countries with various models. This is why I try to underline that I reject this dichotomic approach to things. Indeed, we have to save the system and not cancel it.

It is not only about trade. If somebody is unhappy about the Paris Agreement, about climate change—which is, after all, the future of humankind, isn't it?—one response is to step out; another is to say that we should improve it. Another example is the Intermediate-Range Nuclear Forces Treaty. Some of my generation will remember the mid- and the late '80s. It is likely that one of the important parties does not respect the treaty. We all know that. But is the right solution to cancel it, to step out of it? Perhaps we should just explain to the other party that it has to comply. We have to sit down and explain how the party should comply, explain what new approaches are needed so that the treaty is respected. These are just examples of how, instead of deconstructing existing things, we should perhaps build upon what we have and at the same time improve and reform it. We all have something to do, no doubt. This kind of blaming the other side does not really help. Instead, sitting down and having a dialogue, understanding the changes, including geopolitical structural changes could perhaps help us in mitigating the existing tensions and conflicts, whether this is trade or beyond, and at the same time making the world a safer and more prosperous place.

Thank you for your attention.

Geopolitics and World Trade[1]

For the sake of pith, call them flag and trade. These two shape the world. Flags stand for sovereign states, the political and military power they embody, and the systems of enforcing the interests of that power. Warships bear them. In a way, this what we mean by geopolitics. Taken broadly, trade also means economic activity in general. These two are crucial in shaping what we call the world order, which is subject to much discussion these days. Many say that the world order is changing, and that the process of change is accelerating. Many say the world order is collapsing or will collapse. There is also a debate about what will replace it. I shall limit what I have say to geopolitics and world trade, conceding that they are not the most important factors. A third factor is more important: symbolically, one might call it the Bible, meaning the scriptures, including the Vedas or the Koran. In a broader sense, it implies the concepts mankind has thought up concerning itself. In fact, it is the *Weltgeist* in the Hegelian sense, the spiritual sphere, the world of ideas, culture, the arts, the sciences, and, of course, ideology. It is culture in the broadest sense. This is what really runs the world, but it does so primarily through geopolitics and the world economy.

Let me give two examples in brief. First, currently, technology—namely biotechnology, artificial intelligence, the combination of the two, and whatever follows therefrom—is what determines the world order and will do so

---

[1] Published in: *Magyar Szemle*, volume XXVIII (2019), numbers 5–6, 15–23; and Simai, Mihály and Eszter Lukács (eds.), *Az ENSZ jövője a széteső világban: ENSZ-Akadémia 2020,* Budapest: Magyar ENSZ Társaság, 2020.

in the future. The winner of this increasingly heated technological race will dominate. Now, technology is the work of our minds, science, creativity, and innovation being fundamentally matters of consciousness. Second, the channel through which the intellectual sphere, the *Weltgeist*, determines history is the moral content of this entire system. The question of morality is going to become particularly acute and timely because biotechnology and/or artificial intelligence will confront us with increasingly serious moral problems. These are well-known examples.

The European Commission recently issued its guidelines on the ethical context of artificial intelligence.[2] When I was young, I was fascinated by science fiction literature and reading Ray Bradbury or the Hungarian Péter Kuczka—interestingly enough, both excellent poets. They wrote of many things to come, but many did not come true. We do not know now what is to come, but what we had thought would happen in the far distant future, well, it is now fifty years away. The next fifty years will bring changes that are inestimable, they will accelerate development incredibly and pose very serious new threats and challenges. In his last, posthumous work, the late Stephen Hawking said that the real great risk for humanity is artificial intelligence. That robots will take over power is not a fairy-tale denouement. They may or may not, but humankind is facing a situation it has never seen before.

The two objective factors of world order are therefore geopolitics and world trade. As Carl Schmitt famously said, "*Jede Grundordnung ist eine Raumordnung,*"[3] every basic order is also a spatial order. Geopolitics is called geopolitics because it has a spatial structure in many senses. Order thus always has a structure.

In what follows I shall put forward eight theses, all debatable. They would not be theses if they were irrefutable. In fact, each has but the force of probability. So, all eight theses are debatable and refutable, and arguments can be brought up against each of them. The first three theses are related to the structure of the world order itself.

Thesis one: there is no hierarchy in the structure of the world. Of course, conventional wisdom will say that there is, but in fact, there is no hierarchy.

---

2 Independent High-Level Expert Group on Artificial Intelligence set up by The European Commission: Ethics Guidelines for Trustworthy AI, published 8 April 2019.
3 Carl Schmitt, *Land und Meer: Eine weltgeschichtliche Betrachtung*. Leipzig: Klett-Cotta, [1942] 2018, 71.

Part II

The structure of the world is not hierarchical but heterarchical. Heterarchy is also a system, an order, which does not build up into a vertical, rigid geometric structure. Brain scientists discovered a good seventy or eighty years ago that the human brain has no hierarchy, only heterarchy, and it does have order, "variable ranking." The concept has also appeared in computer science. In terms of the relationship between legal norms, we used to think it was based on the idea that the levels of these norms make up a clear, stable, and hierarchical system. Today, the situation is much more complex, more complicated, there are different nodes, and if you try to place them in space, it turns out that there is no hierarchical system. This first thesis therefore states that there is no hierarchy, but there is a system, one which is variable, and that there are different structures of superiority or subordination in different areas, the actors of which are different.

In the world today, different powers are in the lead in different areas, but none is first in all areas. If we take the most obvious one, GDP, the total amount of domestic product, the structure clearly has two actors. One is the United States, and the other is China. Even so, they are variable, because, as per purchasing power parity, China is first, whereas, on a nominal basis, which is more relevant in world trade, the United States is first. After them come the others, the very important others. If we look at demographics, for instance, also relevant, it is obvious that the first two are China and India, and all the other countries lag far behind them. If we look at nuclear warheads in the world, almost half of them are in Russia, and the other almost half in the United States. There are seven other nuclear powers, and they have a few hundred. North Korea has only twenty, but that can hurt too. The point is that, again, the structure is also different in terms of military power. The heterarchical structure is thus that you have variable factors: military power, demographics, GDP, and trade. Now, the world's first trading power is not China, not the United States, not India, not Japan, but the European Union. The European Union continues to be the world's first factor in terms of both exports and imports.

Thesis two: there is no hegemony. Not only is there no hegemony now but there has never been one, just as there will never be one. Certainly, significant attempts have been made to achieve full-blown global hegemony in history. In the past, global hegemony however could not rise because relations were confined to a specific sphere of the Earth. China, for example, was no rival to the Roman Empire. Later attempts to achieve hegemony, either by land or sea, failed. There indeed was a bipolar world system, and then there was something called the unipolar world system in the early 1990s. But calling it that was a mistake, of course; the world system never was unipolar, but, in any event, the term gained currency in everyday discourse. We no longer talk about it. Today we speak of a multipolar world system, although the poles are not easy to define.

So, there is no hegemon, and there will never be a hegemon, because the existence of a system determined by a single centre also seems to be philosophically impossible. I have no grasp of either particle physics or cosmology, but the impression I gather from the big picture is that there is no system driven by a single centre, nor will there ever be one. When artificial intelligence takes over power, there will be different centres of power within it, which will likewise compete with each other to establish who is faster, whose algorithms are more innovative, who has an edge over the others. Thus, there will never be a single-centre world, officially or unofficially. There is no single secret centre of power. There are multiple centres of power. There are also secret ones, not one but several, all competing with each other.

Thesis three: there are no two systems emerging in the world. The view that the world can be divided into two opposing political, economic, and ideological systems is gaining ground.[4] This does not hold. There are not two systems in the world, there are several. Today, discussions focus on the conflict between China and the United States, a strategic confrontation in different areas and with different means, such as our own main topic, world trade. Undoubtedly, this confrontation is very important, perhaps the most important at the moment, but it cannot be called a conflict between two world systems. It would be interesting to compare the Cold War with the current so-called "cold war" between China and the United States, as some maintain it to be. Although the confrontation between the two powers undeniably bears some of the features of the Cold War, it is different from the struggle between the Western world and the Soviet Union, or, as it was called, "socialism" and capitalism. Both sides had an ideology. (This is the third factor I mentioned!)

---

4   Martin Wolf, "The challenge of one world, two systems." *Financial Times*, 29 January 2019. https://www.ft.com/content/b20a0d62-23b1-11e9-b329-c7e6ceb5ffdf; see also Robert Kagan: "The strongmen strike back." *Washington Post*, 14 March 2019. https://www.washingtonpost.com/news/opinions/wp/2019/03/14/feature/the-strongmen-strike-back/.

China has no coherent ideology. They have the "wangdao," but they themselves cannot define what respect, the deference to superiors, means exactly. Apart from Confucius, they have Mao, with Marx, Lenin, etc., behind. And lately it seems that the powers that be are including Buddha in the line-up. And then there is pragmatism, which is all about production and making lots of money.

Coming back to the structure, there are other major actors who cannot be left out of this game. First, there is Russia. Many say that if there are two systems, Russia belongs to the Chinese one. This is not at all certain. In any event, the Sino-Russian relationship is essentially a pseudo-alliance, which occasionally appears to be a real alliance. There was a period when it was real, until the mid-1950s. Elders will remember the Ussuri incident and its aftermath. There is an extremely long border, which is usually not a very good thing, and then there are fairly moderate economic relations, both in terms of trade and mutual investment. No doubt there are ideological affinities, but these are not that strong, and there is an excess of distrust. It should not be forgotten that China and Russia compare 10 to 1 population-wise, while, in GDP terms, depending on whether we take it at PPP basis or nominally, the ratio is 6 or 8 to 1.

It is crucial that, in this structure, where we deny the existence of two world systems, there are different groups and alliances. These alliances are very often linked to specific, geopolitical and commercial issues or perhaps even matters rooted in consciousness, conception, or ideology. The foundations may vary. The big question is, for example, what holds the Atlantic Alliance together. The Bible? Yes, it remains the most important factor. Undoubtedly, there is thus a common set of values that binds us together, and which can be given different names—the term liberal world order is very fashionable now. What a recent study[5] said about the essential elements of the liberal world order, that it is focused on values and principles and is "rules-based," could be said of a conservative world order. Whatever the case, there is a fundamental commonality of values within the Atlantic Alliance, but there is also a shared geopolitical interest. Both the United States and Europe are more secure if the cohesion of the Atlantic Alliance is maintained, pre-

---

5 Daniel Deudney and G. John Ikenberry: "Liberal World: The Resilient Order," *Foreign Affairs*, volume 97 (2018), number 4, 16–24.

served, and strengthened. We may even have common economic interests. Though it is hard to explain why the United States invokes a national security exception when it imposes trade restrictions on the European Union, its closest ally, let alone on others, such as Canada. The question arises as to whether the determining factor is trade, the economy, or common geopolitical interests, common security, geopolitics boiling down to issues of security. Is then security an existential question or a question of common values?

Thesis four: different areas converge, and their tools are interchanged. For a long time, politicians were either skilled in foreign affairs and geopolitics or in trade, each minding their business. The two naturally interacted, there is nothing strange about that, because commercial and economic interests have always turned into politics and vice versa. But they were two well-defined, separate regimes. Now, however, their tools seem to have been exchanged, the two areas deploying each other's means. The best example of this is still Robert Lighthizer's idea that the United States should invoke as the legal basis for tariff increases not Article XIX of the GATT (providing for safeguard measures applicable in the event of economic disruption and countermeasures against them by the other party) but Article XXI. (Article XXI entitles contracting parties to take any action to restrict trade which they consider necessary for the protection of their essential security interests.) The reason for imposing duties on steel and aluminium products from even the closest allies is that it is in the interest of national security. National security interest is a strange matter. The regime has been in place for a good seventy years, and up to now there has been an unwritten rule that we should try not to invoke it. There was something of a taboo on it; once in a while you broke it, but mostly you respected it. There were two rules to obey. One was not to invoke it; the other one was, if somebody did invoke it, not to dispute it, not to initiate dispute resolution, because the case could never be decided. Professors of law or experts on commerce have no business deciding what the national security interests of a country are or are not.

Now, this regime has been sapped. It has been sapped by the biggest, the dominant actor of the regime. The others are racking their brains what to do. Does the biggest one want to maintain the regime at all? According to all indications, it is not quite keen on doing so, otherwise it would allow the dispute resolution within the WTO framework to operate. But it does not, because it is blocking appointments to the Appellate Body, and if the Appellate

Body is not eked out, it will not be able to decide disputes after a while. There will be no dispute resolution, and if there is no dispute resolution, norms and regulations are in vain, as there is no enforcement of them. The question arises whether it is the whole regime that is at stake, or only parts of it.

The United States imposed restrictions on the basis of Article XXI of the GATT, wanting to deal with a commercial, economic problem by recourse to national security. (Whether it is dealing soundly with the economic problem itself is a debatable economic question.) There is a tiny country which has decided that it can do likewise. It imposed one-hundred-percent additional tariffs first on Serbian and then on Bosnian and Herzegovinan products. The country is not recognized by all, and it is called Kosovo. And what does it refer to? National security. When asked what national security has to do with the hundred percent tariff, they answer that Serbia continues to block Kosovo's recognition in international organizations. Now, this is a vital issue for them, directly affecting their national security. If the biggest can do it, the smallest can try. The hundred percent tariff is still in force. The entire system is being unravelled, and its spatial structure and geometry are being loosened up.

Thesis five: bilateral relationships are never closed. There is no pure bilateralism, there never has been and never will be. First, trade is inherently multilateral. This was invented by neither politicians nor lawyers; trade was multilateral long before Adam Smith's time, because a particular type of English fabric bought by the Portuguese for tailoring into clothes was then sold to a third country. And in the world of supply and value chains, it is quite obvious that the moment there is an intervention—a restriction is imposed or a special concession is granted, or a bilateral free trade agreement entered into—the impact ripples out to all actors involved. There is no better example to the butterfly effect than world trade. This is why GATT came into being at the beginning, and this is why it was continued in the World Trade Organization; it was clear that, at the level of legal norms, the regime could only be grasped in a multilateral framework. This was the basis of the multilateral most-favoured-nation treatment principle. This was why the most-favoured-nation treatment, which had been applied in a bilateral framework for a long time, had to be multilateralized. And that was why the special rules—the *erga omnes* principle, that if a measure is taken against one, it must be taken against all—had to introduced, subject to rare exception. In vain is action taken solely against A, because it will affect B, C, and D. The legal regulation therefore grasped only this obvious element of reality. The restrictions the US imposed on China so far affect imports worth USD 302 billion. According to an UNCTAD study, out of the USD 302 billion in imports, goods worth USD 250 billion were diverted. The restriction thus does not protect the industry it was meant to protect, because someone else will import the same products. The restrictions benefitted the European Union—its agriculture and car industries—to the tune of USD 70 billion, but Canada, Mexico and others also profited from the resulting diversion.

Thus, whatever restriction someone imposes, its impact ripples across the whole system. This was what the multilateral regulatory regime tried to deal with, but it now seems to be on its last legs. The question is whether at least its essence can be salvaged.

Thesis six: globalization is slowing down, which is also related to the previous thesis. It is not accelerating but slowing down. Figures on world trade clearly substantiate this. For a long time, we observed, the dynamics of world trade exceeded the dynamics of global output, or GDP growth. This was always the case in the past; we grew up in its midst, but it has not been the case for the last five to six years. The main reason for this is technological advance: things need not be physically transported, it is enough to transmit the data and manufacture the goods on the spot, for example, with 3D technology. The structure of world trade is changing dramatically. At first, we traded mostly goods, then, increasingly, services, but now we trade more and more data. Legal regulation needs to capture this data flow, which is no easy task. Especially when the whole world is going to be made up of data, and perhaps we humans may no longer be the ones processing the data. Things are changing, and technology is driving not so much globalization in the traditional sense but rather the localization of production, bringing work back to where it had been taken away from. There are other reasons as well, sustainability in particular.

The way world trade is related to sustainability is subject to fascinating debates. WTO Director General Roberto Azevêdo said he had never heard of the two being linked, but they are. By moving goods around, we pollute the sea and the air, our footprint on this wretched planet is getting bigger. Not to mention the fact that free trade can, in some cases, help us move production that is no longer regarded as appropriate at home for environmental reasons to where it still is. So, there is a correlation. The other issue is that this should be addressed by regulating trade, not restricting it. Sustainability is thus coming into focus, and it is likewise deaccelerating globalization. Globalization is gradually slowing down, at least in certain segments, and is being replaced by regionalization. The slowdown in globalization does not mean that growth has to slacken and welfare to decline. Regionalization is gaining momentum. Distance matters. Just-in-time delivery in the supply chain means that car parts, for instance, must arrive at a given hour, not later, which requires the close geographical proximity of production facilities linking up.

There are also geopolitical reasons behind regionalization. Every regional free trade agreement (RTA) has geopolitical considerations to it. Some can be influenced even by economic philosophy, ultimately intellectual and ideological concerns. All these factors lead to regionalization. The British will have a lot to say about this in five or ten years' time, when it dawns on them that they had been fooled by the illusion of "Global Britain" and that their trade with Australia, Canada, and New Zealand could never make up for the loss of trade with their neighbours. Moreover, we, the European Union, have free trade agreements with these countries, and it will not be easy for the British join in. But Australia will never take the place of France. One need only take a look at the map, and, of course, at history and culture.

Though bilateral relationships being never closed, regionalization means that regional linkages are reinforced. There are currently 471 Regional Free Trade Agreements (RTAs) in effect, or to be more precise, this is the number member states notified to the WTO committee responsible. This is the number notified, but many more have been entered into, and the number is growing. The European Union, of course, has the largest number of these agreements in the world—more than forty—but these cover more than a hundred countries, such as the Cotonou regime with its many members. Others have also concluded such agreements, the United States nineteen, China seventeen; and the competition is on, negotiations are under way, the actors being aware of the fact that the multilateral system is not going to develop any further and that its future is uncertain. Although there are attempts to move in a plurilateral direction, meaning "many but not all" (e-commerce, etc.), there are strong barriers to progress. The argument for strengthening regional frameworks is that those party to them enjoy advantages, while those who are not face disadvantages.

The European Union is again negotiating with the United States. This is perhaps the most important issue for Europe today. We have concluded an agreement with Japan, which is a huge achievement, covering 30 percent of the global output. It is unprecedented in all the world, and perhaps we have not celebrated it enough. We have also concluded an agreement with Canada, and there have been disputes arising from that, and we will shortly have a ruling from the European Court of Justice on its provisions on investment disputes.[6] As one of the results of the agreement with Canada, Canadian lobster will enter the European Union duty-free. In the United States, the best lobster is sold in restaurants and even lobster shacks along highways in Maine. Maine is a small state up in the northeast corner, bordering Canada. Maine lobster can only get to Europe under a high tariff, Canadian lobster is duty free. This is good for Maine lobsters but not for lobster farmers. The United States therefore says let us negotiate but let us include agriculture and fisheries in the agreement. Our position, on the other hand, is that agriculture and fisheries were not included in the Trump–Juncker deal.

Interestingly, the US are now invoking GATT rules, saying that Article XXIV requires that FTAs must cover all or substantially all trade. This would affect more than 90 percent of tariff lines, but there is no clear case law. Americans happen to say that there is a multilateral set of rules we have to abide by, and we have to include agriculture. We Hungarians said the same thing to the European Community in 1991, arguing that under Article XXIV of the GATT our association (free trade) agreement should also cover agriculture. Currently, the American position is that if we do not include agriculture, there will be trouble. In any case, the European Union has now significantly increased its imports of soybeans—this is the diversion effect I mentioned above—because as China in response does not import American soya, it ends up in Europe, and we buy them. The European Union is not a "country conducting state trade" like China; the market decides what we buy. But we have passed legislation at EU level which says that soybeans can now be used to produce bioenergy. And, of course, if there is such legislation, importers will immediately start buying American soybeans.

---

6   On 30 April 2019, the European Court of Justice announced its ruling that the mechanism for the resolution of disputes between investors and States provided for by the free trade agreement between the EU and Canada (CETA) is compatible with EU law.

So, there is a race to conclude free trade agreements, dropping out of which is out of the question. There might be countries for which this is less relevant. Russia, for example, sells fuels, natural gas and oil. It also sells missile systems, but tariffs do not really matter even for these. Theirs is a special situation, but Russians know that free trade is important. When they are approached to conclude a free trade agreement, their answer is that such an agreement can be concluded with the Eurasian Economic Union, the customs union of the Russian Federation, the Kyrgyz Republic, the Republic of Belarus, the Republic of Kazakhstan, and the Republic of Armenia. One of the differences between a customs union and a free trade agreement is that the members of the customs union cannot conclude a free trade agreement independently, because they are bound by the regime, the tariff and other rules of the customs union.

The Brexit deadlock boils down to the customs union conundrum. Customs union or no customs union? Before the referendum was called, British voters should have been asked one question, the saving question in exams in international economic law: what is the difference between a free trade agreement and a customs union? If the examinee knows the right answer, he passes; if he does not, he fails. Well, it seems that a good number of decision makers did not know the right answer, and perhaps many of them still cannot tell the difference. Moreover, they neither know that, for all free trade, all imported automotive products can be stopped at the border because the rules of origin have to be checked. What is at stake at the moment is whether the agreement we have with Japan, which came into force on 1 February, is going to be immediately extended to the UK or not. What is going to happen with the rules of origin? Currently, whatever the twenty-eight of us produce qualifies as European goods on the basis of cumulation. For the Japanese, this is of no interest, because they are alone and meet the rules of origin alone. But if the British leave, will they meet the rules of origin alone? Among others, these issues were not considered beforehand.

Thesis seven: competition is heating up, which is not a particularly new thing to say. What is competition about? Above all, it is about technology. Commercial competition is also ultimately about technology: Who gets the edge in technology? Who is going to lead in artificial intelligence, in biotechnology, and in combining the two? In any case, this is the central question of the current competition. But this is the crucial question also from the point of view of security policy and defence, for it can decide conflicts and topple the well-established principles of mutual deterrence, which has worked more or less well so far. The other very serious challenge is that if a social stratum can afford to use the special tools of biotechnology and take advantage of their benefits, it will create unprecedented inequality. This may lead to a qualitative leap and a risk of social upheaval that humanity may no longer be able to manage. The race is therefore also for advantages, with the gap between winners and losers widening. That is why new tools emerge, and why we adopt the tools of other, unfamiliar areas. And in doing so, we warp the system further, which continues to wither, to become increasingly fluid and diffuse, itself increasing risks.

Thesis eight: dangers worsen. Some say this has to do with the phenomenon of entropy which the whole world is subject to. Perhaps they are right; yet there is harmony too. The vast majority of dangers are human made. Most of the global risks we face we brought about. This also means that our will and action, the rules we make and respect, can and must help. There have been examples where this was successful. The situation is thus by no means hopeless.

Book-launch Talk for *The Regional World Order: Transregionalism, Regional Integration, and Regional Projects across Europe and Asia*[1]

Delivered at the National University of Public Service, 17 December 2019 to launch.[2]

This is a timely book. We have long been discussing and writing about the growing fragmentation, regionalization, and localization process that has been taking place alongside and also as a result of the elusive globalization syndrome. These processes are not mutually exclusive, to which there is nothing new. There have been globalization processes before; in the Roman Empire, you paid in sestertii from Spain to the Danube, though the system would fragment later. The first great period of globalization in the history of the world's economy took place at the end of the nineteenth century and the beginning of the twentieth century, when a truly global and multilateral world economic and trading system was established. The legal technique was different, because bilateral yet interlinked trade agreements created an essentially unified regulatory framework, which would be followed by a really multilateral legal regime from 1947 on. Set down in bilateral agreements previously, the most-favoured-nation treatment became multilateral. The *Corpus Juris Hungarici* included a large number of bilateral trade and shipping agreements, each of which granted the other party most-favoured-nation

---

[1] Alexei D. Voskressenski and Boglárka Koller (eds.), *The Regional World Order: Transregionalism, Regional Integration, and Regional Projects across Europe and Asia*. Lenham, Boulder, New York, and London: Lexington, 2019.
[2] Published in *Európai Tükör*, volume 23 (2020), number 1, 137–142.

treatment. This would then be upset by a period of intense fragmentation: the First World War. The world economy tried to straighten things out again, but it did not have much time, because 1929 brought about new problems. Later, in 1947, the legal framework known as the Bretton Woods regime came into being, creating a truly multilateral, open, and inclusive system of trade regulation.

In this light, I was all the more struck by Charles Ziegler's statement in *The Regional World Order* that the General Agreement on Tariffs and Trade (GATT) was a piece of closed regionalism, a *fortress arrangement* that curbed global economic relations (page 186). The GATT was the exact opposite of all this. It was open from the outset, to the extent that it included Czechoslovakia and Poland, although these two countries were subsequently banned from it by the Soviet Union. Obtaining home rule and independence, developing countries progressively joined the GATT, which now has 164 members, including Russia and China. The WTO, the World Trade Organization, is now a truly universal international organization.

Another misunderstanding that appears in the book is that the WTO is the successor to the GATT. There are two problems here. First, the GATT was never an organization, it was an agreement. It still is an agreement. On the other hand, it has no successor because it still exists. It has not been terminated. There can only be a successor to something that has ceased to exist. GATT 1947 is still in force today as part of GATT 1994. GATT 1994 consists of several parts, first and foremost the 1947 text. This text is still in force today, and it is on the basis of this text that we will be discussing, for example, in connection with the British withdrawal, what conditions are to be met in order that the agreement is in line with the multilateral system and particularly with Article XXIV of the GATT. So nothing has replaced the GATT, but the system has been expanded. And GATT 1994, as we now call it, is the cardinal or central element of a substantially enlarged system and of a number of related agreements, from trade in services to intellectual property. I say this only because I cannot find an explanation for how the most open and inclusive multilateral trading system in the world can be called a closed *fortress arrangement*.

Of course, we know perfectly well that GATT 1994 has serious problems. For example, it is not developing. It made huge progress in 1995 but has not moved forward for at least fifteen years. This is one of the reasons—by no means the only reason—why the structure of world-trade regulation is becoming regionalized, which is the subject matter of this book. One after the other, regional and bilateral trade agreements, known as Free Trade Agreements (FTAs) or Preferential Trade Agreements (PTAs), are being concluded whereby parties grant each other preferential treatment as opposed to general treatment. This is why *favour* and *preference* should be distinguished; after all, they do not mean the same. A *favour* is (most) favoured treatment, which is granted to all those party to the multilateral system; while a *preference* can only be obtained on the basis of a separate bilateral or a multilateral (regional) trade agreement. The most commonly used term today is RTA (Regional Trade Agreement). Their number is growing rapidly, and this is both a cause and a consequence of fragmentation, that is, the creation of smaller, largely regional entities.

First generation RTAs were content to break down barriers to trade. It later became clear that if barriers to trade were to be removed, a level playing field had to be created (for example, in the area of state-aid rules), and that there was a need to approximate the most diverse protection regimes and harmonize different regulations and rules. This will be the big debate between the European Union and the United Kingdom over the next eleven months. It will be necessary to clarify what the parties mean by a *level playing field* and to establish some level of regulatory harmonization. This is what the British are not so keen on doing, especially given that they will have to choose between European and US regulations. Free trade agreements now also have an increasingly broad regulatory content. The book illustrates very well the huge differences between different regional types of regulation in this area.

A great virtue of the book is, I think, its new approach to the subject matter. It introduces the new category of transregional relations, where the formal, legal elements of relations between regions do not appear, as opposed to institutionalized interregional relations. An example of the latter would be the agreement between the European Union and Mercosur—insofar as it does come into being in spite of all odds against it. As far as the EU–ASEAN agreement is concerned, the European Union's decision was to conclude agreements with each of the member states of ASEAN first. Some of these are already in place—with, for example, Singapore and Vietnam. Once all are concluded, then comes the geopolitical and trade regulatory dilemma of how to transform this web into a single interregional agreement. We have not reached that stage yet; we do not even know when we will, but the scholarly analyses provided by this book will obviously assist this work.

A more difficult question is how relations between the European Union and the Eurasian Economic Union (EEU) should develop. After various transitional formations, the latter reached the level of establishing a customs union; it has an institutional system and can operate at international level. In principle, it can conclude interregional agreements. Recently, a number of rather naïve, politically motivated ideas have surfaced in Hungarian public discourse in this regard, and thus it is opportune to refer to certain basic facts. The EEU has a total nominal GDP of 1.7 trillion US dollars, equal to or slightly less than that of Italy. Its GDP at purchasing power parity is much more, 4.7 trillion US dollars. The big difference between the two is because the EEU countries have very low standards of living, and because their nominal GDP is volatile, as exchange rate movements—mostly that of the Russian rouble—have strongly impacted it. Russia accounts for 87 percent of the GDP of the EEU, which has a budget that is 1 percent of that of the EU. The budget of the African Union is five times that of the EEU. There is thus room for improvement.

More importantly, Russia has little real interest in concluding a classical, traditional free-trade agreement facilitating the export of industrial goods. Its accession to the GATT took a long time and involved several difficulties, some of which remain. Exporting energy, gas, and oil does not require free trade; those that need oil and gas will buy it. The strength of the Russian economy rests on two factors: the sale of energy and arms. If a county buys arms, it will not be of a mind to impose a tariff on the source. The point is to buy the most modern, most efficient, and preferably—as is often the case—the most expensive weapons systems. These products are thus not subject to traditional trade regulation.

It is very well that the EEU has come into being, but dreams that we will join it, because the future belongs to the vast Asian mainland, are unfounded. It is an open question whether the source of dominance is on the seas or on land. In any case, China does not wish to decide this question, because it is going to drive the Belt and Road Initiative through both land and sea, both Central Asia and the Indian Ocean. That is how it will arrive at Piraeus, which is important for us, because Chinese goods will travel en masse from there via the Belgrade–Budapest high-speed rail link, cheaply and quickly.

Part II

When the multilateral system was set up back in 1947, it was already seen that, although the system proclaimed the principle of equal treatment, which would be put into practice by the ingenious legal technique of most-favoured-nation treatment, exceptions would have to be made. The main rule is the most-favoured-nation principle, but Article XXIV already provides for exceptions, free trade and customs union. Then, after a few decades, the need to give preferences to developing countries arose, and that is how the Generalized System of Preferences (GSP) was introduced.

Having been with us for a long time, fragmentation, regionalization, and localization have recently intensified. This is reflected in trends in world trade, investment, and capital flows. World trade has not grown faster than the world economy for many years, especially in the area of trade in goods. The structure of trade is also changing, as trade in goods is declining relative to trade in services. It has turned out that maritime transport is the most damaging sector in terms of climate change, as its ecological footprint is the highest. Free trade is a good thing, but the footprint of trade must be reduced. If we regionalize the entire system and network of connections, we inevitably look for closer sourcing and sales opportunities. Free-trade agreements themselves represent this regionalization and are therefore both cause and effect of this transformation.

There are four reasons and conditions for establishing free-trade agreements. The first is the intensity of trade and economic relations between the parties. The second is that there should be some similarity in levels of economic development. This is not always the case because, for example, ASEAN includes the richest country in the world, Brunei, and also the poorest countries in the world, Laos, Cambodia, and Myanmar. Yet this is the regional economic integration that has so far reached the highest level after the European Union. A third condition is that there should be a minimum level of similarity in economic philosophies and, accordingly, economic policies. In practice, this means that all the parties must be parties to the GATT, because then at least the main principles are accepted. Many a country seeks to conclude a regional agreement with China, and quite a few have already done so. One of the main questions for the future is how Chinese dominance will be enforced through regional systems, particularly in the Indian Ocean, the Pacific, and Central Asia. However, China is still—some would argue, increasingly—a foreign body in the GATT, and this is a major source of problems. Trump is not the only one responsible for the breakdown of a system that has worked well for seventy years. One of the main reasons for the problems is that China has never considered itself fully bound by the core principles of the GATT. Where the allocation of financial resources is in the hands of a banking system controlled by a political committee of a single party, it is difficult to talk about the market economy that the GATT presupposes. The dominant role of state-owned enterprises and issues concerning intellectual property are also grounds for complaints by the Americans and, increasingly, the Europeans.

The fourth condition is the geographical distance between the parties. Countries that are closer to each other tend to find it easier to establish regional alliances and economic integration, either in the form of free trade or customs unions. *Distance matters*, as the dictum has it. It remains to be seen whether Australia, New Zealand, and the United States can replace the European Union, where 50 percent of British exports currently go, and where a majority of *supply chains* require *in-time delivery*. Only the future can tell.

The greatest strength of *The Regional World Order* is that it raises the fundamental question: What is first, security or the economy? And what is the role of the third factor: ideology? This is what we now call identity. How do they relate to one another? Geopolitics has entered the system of free-trade agreements. On the one hand, it destroys and dismantles existing systems, on the other, it builds new ones. Geopolitical interests have contributed to the establishment of free-trade agreements and/or customs unions based on Article XXIV of the GATT and their upgraded versions, which go far beyond their original purposes, covering the environment, climate change, human rights, and much more.

Regional cooperation regimes outside Europe tend to pay little attention to the legal structure. They do not build institutional structures or mechanisms for settling legal disputes. Their security-policy dimension is stronger. The future will decide whether or not they move towards a more robust institutional set-up. ASEAN, for example, is moving in this direction, and perhaps the USMCA, the replacement of NAFTA, also.

There are also examples in Europe of cooperation without an institutional make-up, and the book includes an excellent study on them. The Visegrád Group is doing very well, and we have no intention of creating an institutional framework for it at the moment. Visegrád cooperation has increasingly made its presence felt. At first, it was just a distraction for some, but we are now in a next phase, and have become a serious factor. In the last few weeks at least, it seemed that no really important personnel decisions for the top EU positions could be taken without us.

The reason why it is important to analyse the relationship between security and economic regulation is that one of the ways to dismantle a multilateral trading system is that security policy is, on the one hand, a means of pursuing economic and commercial interests and on the hand is a means of concealing them. This is the case when the national security exception under Article XXI of the GATT is invoked to restrict imports of steel and aluminium from Europe, Mexico, Japan, and Canada. The national security exception is difficult to bring to dispute settlement, although, as a result of the ruling in the Rosneft case between Russia and Ukraine, the issue could in principle be subject to dispute settlement, but, as of 10 December 2019, dispute settlement has essentially terminated. Failing to have its members replaced, the WTO's Appellate Body has ceased to exist, which means that if a party appeals a first-instance panel decision, no binding decision shall be made in the absence of an appeal body, and the appeal will be an *"appeal to the void"*. The system–which has been in place since 1947, was strengthened in 1995, and has functioned quite well– is now ostensibly being undone.

As for the dispute settlement procedures of regional agreements, they also rely heavily on multilateral rules. If there is thus no multilateral system, it will be more difficult for regional systems to solve their own problems. The point of this book is that, in the absence of a multilateral system, it is possible to build a world order that no longer has a universal multilateral framework and instead build something new in its place. For instance, a plurilateral system might be considered with many members, almost all but not all. It could exclude, for example, the United States. This would be a knotty matter; a dangerous one too—just think of the political and geopolitical consequences. Would Europe exclude its closest ally? The guardian of its security?

Perhaps the most important question regarding the emerging world order is the extent to which the world is fragmenting and regionalizing, and what its geopolitical, security, economic, and trade policy consequences will be. This is the subject of this book, which deserves special attention and is of particular value. One might agree or disagree with its findings and conclusions, but the authors' contribution to understanding the major processes that will shape our future is indisputable.

Part III
Still Europe...

The Visegrád Group, Central Europe, and the European Union[1]

Hungarian financier, thinker, and erstwhile State Secretary for Finance Elemér Hantos founded an organization in Vienna in 1925 that he called the *Mitteleuropäische Wirtschaftstagung* or *Congrès économique de l'Europe centrale*, i.e., Central European Economic Conference. Its aim was to build stronger economic cooperation and integration among the successor states of the dismantled Austro-Hungarian Monarchy, and thus gradually restore the economic unity that had worked well for decades in terms of trade, transport, infrastructure, and so on. The objective was therefore essentially economic. Geographically, it was meant to cover the successor states at first, i.e., Austria, Hungary, Czechoslovakia, Romania, and Yugoslavia. It was meant to be open to the possibility that this Central European integration might later expand towards Germany or possibly even further. Elemér Hantos envisioned first an exchange rate stabilization, then the gradual introduction of a single currency, to be followed by a customs union. Interestingly, the sequence he imagined was contrarywise to what actually took place in European integration.

In Hantos's concept, infrastructural developments, the integration of rail and river transport, and the centralization of postal services were the third area of economic integration.

It was also in 1925 that an Austrian count called Richard Coudenhove-Kalergi founded the much better-known Paneuropean Union with the aim of creating a politically united Europe. The *Mitteleuropäische* idea was essen-

---

[1] Originally published in Angéla Balaskó (ed.), *Szakpolitikai együttműködés a V4-en belül, Visegrád magyar kormányzati szemmel*. Budapest: Külügyi és Külgazdasági Intézet, 2018, 83–96.

tially rooted in the economy, while the Paneuropean Union had a political objective, and Richard Coudenhove-Kalergi believed that it was to be based on Franco-German reconciliation, and this would grow into pan-European political cooperation or even union.

Various national sections of the Paneuropean Union were set up, including the Hungarian one, of which Elemér Hantos was of course a member. The geographical space was thus different, the starting point was also different, but there was common ground. However, the two concepts, the two ideas, competed with each other. When Elemér Hantos was asked what he actually wanted, central European cooperation or European, pan-European integration, his answer was that the essentially economic integration of Central Europe advocated by his *Mitteleuropäische Wirtschaftstagung* should come about first, and then be extended. Germany would obviously be the first target, followed by a pan-European cooperation with some regional ramifications. Central European cooperation should therefore retain its own identity, but there should also be a Western European group, basically involving Germany, France, Belgium, and Luxembourg, and possibly a Baltic and Scandinavian group. Ultimately, Elemér Hantos envisioned a regionalized pan-Europe, which would achieve the ultimate goal of the Coudenhove-Kalergi Paneuropean Union, the creation of a politically united Europe.

History buried all these ideas. First, the rise of Nazi Germany in the early 1930s, then the Second World War, and then a world order that brushed aside the ideas of creating either Central European or pan-European cooperation. Another important event took place in 1951: the conclusion of the Treaty of Paris establishing the European Coal and Steel Community.

Then came a major event that would have a decisive impact on developments in Europe and globally: the Hungarian uprising in 1956. It made it clear far and wide that the Soviet threat was tangible, not a distant abstract geopolitical category but a real one to be reckoned with. Later, the quashing of the Prague Spring in 1968 would reinforce this message. Undoubtedly, the process of realizing the vision of European integration was significantly accelerated by our 1956 revolution.

At the time of the 1989–90 regime-change, we did not know much about Elemér Hantos; Coudenhove-Kalergi was slightly better known. But we were all soon confronted with the fundamental question of whether we primarily wanted Central European cooperation or accession to European integration.

The answer at the time was quite clearly in favour of the second option. However, we also considered it very important to establish, or, if you wish, revive Central European cooperation. In the opinion of many, this was largely the result of external factors. We primarily wanted to facilitate our European and Euro-Atlantic integration. But in terms of external factors, apart from Brussels we must also mention Moscow as well, because one of the primary objectives was to dismantle the older structures, the Comecon and the Warsaw Pact. This dual objective required cooperation among "post-communist" Central European countries.

But beyond that, there was a much more important and much deeper reason. These countries faced a historic choice. They had to decide which tradition, which heritage they wanted to follow. Did they want to continue the culture of confrontation that had been repressed and subsumed in the previous decades, did they want to go on with their tensions and conflicts, or did they want to create a new culture, principally one of cooperation and collaboration. The answer was absolutely clear and historic; they chose the latter. They decided to move towards a culture of cooperation. Multilateral cooperation would also be a way of alleviating existing conflicts, tensions, and the more difficult aspects of our historical heritage in the framework of bilateral relations. This idea would later be put into practice.

Hence the conclusion that the Visegrád cooperation was in fact but the turning of an intellectual, cultural, and spiritual notion, a kind of Central European identity, into political and economic cooperation. In any case, if we want to define Central Europe, we cannot do so on a geographical basis, because we do not know exactly where its borders run. The Swiss also claim to be Central Europeans, and we have not yet mentioned the possible northern or southern outposts. (For example, the wider cooperation called the Central European Initiative grew to eventually have a total of seventeen members.)

If we therefore want to grasp the essence of Central Europe, we must look for it in the intellectual, cultural, and spiritual spheres. What is its essence? First of all, that Central Europe is part of Europe. It bears all the elements and qualities that Europe bears, but a little more densely, a little more intensely, at a slightly higher speed. There is still more religion, there are more languages, more historically inherited tensions, and thus more pressure to live together. Crosses have different shapes here, and, before the Holocaust, this is where most synagogues stood. There is a lot of anxiety here, a lot of unease. There is a lot of melancholy but also a lot of humour. We have a lot of complexes, including an inferiority-turned-superiority complex. At the same time, there is a special ingenuity, a special creativity. All these belong to the essence of a Central European identity based on a common cultural heritage.

The Visegrád cooperation has been a success story for more than a quarter of a century. There have been setbacks, but, overall, this cooperation has stood the tests of the times. Almost half of these twenty-five years were spent outside the European Union, and then, on 1 May 2004, we seemingly returned to the dichotomy of Central Europe and pan-Europe. After we all became members of the European Union, the question arose of what to do with our Central European cooperation, what to do with the Visegrád Group. There were even voices saying that this cooperation had already fulfilled its task and was no longer needed.

There was another important element of Central European cooperation: the Central European Free Trade Agreement, which had in fact been a realization of part of Elemér Hantos's vision of economic integration. It was obvious that, after the winding up of Comecon, which had never functioned as a multilateral trading system, something had to be done, since trade- and economic relations among the Central European countries were weak. Had we burdened them with the usual customs duties and other trade barriers, these countries would have withered away completely. Consequently, we had to move very quickly and conclude a free-trade agreement. Incidentally, this would be suggested to us years later as an alternative to EU membership. Even political actors of consequence in Western Europe were surprized when, thanking them for their advice, we informed them that we had already concluded such an agreement. Finally, on 1 May 2004, the Central European Free Trade Agreement ceased to apply in the Visegrád Group, as it no longer made sense. But the Visegrád cooperation continued to do so.

The Visegrád Group held together and gained strength. It dawned on us that it could give us clout, a new ability to enforce the economic and political interests of our region within the framework of integration, the European Union. And so it did. The Visegrád cooperation has therefore been successful in this respect as well, and it remains so to this day. The example brought up most often is the drafting process of the multiannual financial framework, where the initial idea had been much less favourable for the countries of Central Europe than the one finally adopted. As a result of their well-coordinated, well-organized cooperation, these countries benefitted the most, especially in the allocation of the cohesion funds. Hungary perhaps did best in this regard.

Of course, there were or could have been conflicts of interest, since we had to share a certain budget. However, we staved off conflicts of interest and always sought common ground, striving to achieve a common result beneficial to all. There was such a strong sense of commonality among the Visegrád Group that even when our objective interests ostensibly diverged—for example, in the case of the common agricultural policy—we managed to cooperate, our common interests being fundamentally more important. What we thus share is much more than an economic interest bound to a specific moment in time.

Tests came later. The Russian aggression and everything that happened thereafter were undoubtedly a major divisive factor within the Visegrád cooperation, especially between Poland and Hungary. Many have said that history has returned. In this context, the mainstream Western press has repeatedly buried the Visegrád cooperation, which, by the way, it had barely taken note of before. At least the conflict has drawn attention to us, and we have been noticed. In reality, the Visegrád Group has withstood this test well, and it has become clear that the differences in sensitivities, security policy, and economic interests can always be bridged, and appropriate compromises can and must be reached.

The return of history has also brought along with it a further element: an extraordinary reappreciation of the Central European region in geopolitical and security terms. We had been forgotten, regarded as being of no consequence. The occupation of Crimea and half or a third of the eastern Ukrainian provinces by predominantly external forces made the world realize that this region is important after all. The Baltics and Poland felt an imminent threat, which also brought the region into focus.

The immigration crisis has also drawn the world's attention to the fact that Central Europe is united for some reason beyond specific economic and political interests. This factor of strong cohesion is difficult for outsiders to understand. The immigration crisis has had, and will obviously continue to have, many negative consequences. But it has certainly made us and the world aware of our cohesion. We are often accused of thinking that the European Union is but a common cash cow, a payment office for picking up money. It turns out that the opposite is true. For some reason, these countries consider their European cultural heritage and identity the most important, the existence of which is clear even if national identity precedes it.

The reason for this is that the European character and identity of the Central European region has been under attack from the outside. Two-thirds of the Hungarian population was lost during the Mongolian invasion, and we fought against the Ottoman Empire for two hundred years while the nations of Western Europe were busy fighting wars against each other, the Hundred Years' War, the Thirty Years' War, and were less subject to external threat. On the frontiers, we knew that if we lost our Christian European identity, we would lose our national identity and even our very existence. So national identity and European identity, the link with Europe, were, and still are, closely intertwined in our case. That is why the European cultural heritage is so important for us, and why we stand up for it more outspokenly.

The next challenge after the immigration crisis was the British Brexit referendum, which has at least two implications for Central European cooperation and Central Europe in general. One is that we have lost an ally. The other is that it has led to a very pronounced revaluation of the region, both economically and geopolitically. The focus of European integration has been shifting eastwards for twenty-five years; after all, it began with German unification. A symbolic expression of this was the relocation of the German capital from Bonn to Berlin.

Now, this process is continuing; due to Brexit, Germany will inevitably turn more strongly towards Central Europe, the economic and intellectual resources of the Visegrád market of sixty-five million people. Consequently, the focus of European integration as a whole is shifting eastwards even more, and Central Europe will thus become more valuable. This will be another major consequence of Brexit for the region.

It is a serious dilemma that, although the Visegrád Group is the most visible, efficient, and successful form of Central European cooperation, it is not the same as Central Europe in geographical, intellectual, cultural, or historical terms. Central Europe is a wider, broader region and concept. The position of the Visegrád Four is that this informal cooperation cannot be formally extended to include other countries. This is a dilemma that needs to be resolved. The solution is to shape a special partnership with the countries of the region, i.e., the Central European countries, the "neighbours." Insofar as they express their willingness, these countries should be treated as distinct from one another within the so-called V4+ circle that currently exists. They are special, regional, Central European partners, who should be given special status. That said, of course, the V4+ formula, which we have developed significantly in recent years, should be continued. The Visegrád Four have been put on the stage of world politics. Many important countries have expressed their interest in meeting with representatives of the Visegrád Group: India, China, Japan, Turkey, etc. So V4+ cooperation is working well, but it would be useful to highlight and treat the neighbours, the countries in the immediate region, the Central European countries, separately.

But there are further dilemmas. We talk a lot about a common energy policy, creating a secure energy supply in Central Europe, the backwardness of the infrastructure in Central Europe, and the undeveloped North–South system, lagging far behind Western Europe. We talk a lot but have done less. We had once organized a cycling race between Budapest and Kraków to prove that it is faster to get from the former to the latter by bicycle than rail. Another problem is that our Central European capital markets are isolated from each other and fragmented. There is a lot to be done here too.

Central European countries still have a long way to go in the overall catching-up process. Our growth rate is faster than is the European average. Yet, more and more people are suggesting that we have fallen into the so-called middle-income trap, and that it is therefore absolutely necessary to assume a better position on the value chain. This would also enable us to raise our extremely low domestic wages. The secret to a better position on the value chain is science, research, development, innovation, and education. All the countries of the Visegrád Group and Central Europe should concentrate their resources in this area above all. The most valuable part of the value chain is not the end but the beginning, or rather before the beginning. The best thing is to come up with an idea, then to produce the basic materials, then the semi-finished products, and last to assemble them. But first you have to invent the new product, the new service. That is why intellectual property rights are of such enormous importance in the world today, because whoever invents the product will receive a significant part of the revenue from the sale of the product. And if we want to invent something, we need science, scientists, and innovation.

We also have geopolitical dilemmas, and how to relate to the two major powers near us, Germany and Russia, is of immense importance. It must be underlined: there is no equal distance. We are members of the European Union and the Atlantic Alliance. Germany is our ally. We are not intermediaries. Neither are we bumpers—nor clutch discs. We belong to one side, and we are of course interested in much better cooperation between Europe and Russia than we have at the moment, interested in a stable, predictable political and economic environment in every sense of the word. From this point of view, too, the unity of the Visegrád Group is crucial. In order to preserve the unity of Central Europe at all times, which is particularly important to the outside world, we need common-sense compromises so that we can strengthen this particular brand here in the region and throughout the world.

An ancient curse of this region is that we have always curried favour with outside powers. We tried to settle our disputes by running to the great powers—any power, French, British, German or other—and winning their support. Now, if we have disputes among ourselves, we thank others for their advice, but let them know that we can settle our differences among ourselves and need no outside "great power" assistance. In this respect, too, there has been significant progress over the last twenty-five years.

The Visegrád Group is Central Europe's most significant and successful cooperation, Central Europe is an increasingly important and influential factor in European integration, and Europe's fate is increasingly influenced by global economic and geopolitical developments. The cooperation of the Visegrád Group and Central Europe has therefore taken place within the framework of European integration and global processes and will continue to do so in the years and decades to come.

The debate on European integration, and more specifically on the future of the European Union, has in fact been going on ever since the integration process started and even before. The circumstances and conditions change, but the fundamental issues are essentially the same. To what extent do the Member States confer the exercise of the competences arising from their sovereignty on the integration institutions, i.e., to what extent do they exercise them jointly? A further question is how these competences conferred are exercised by the Community, and subsequently by the EU institutions, i.e., whether decisions are made by unanimity or qualified majority voting. Related to the scope of conferred competences, the next question is to what extent differences can be accepted within the scopes of the competences conferred on the Community and EU institutions, i.e., within the single, integrated system, either at the level of individual Member States or of groups of Member States, i.e., to what extent and in what ways historical, geographical, economic, security policy, and—not least—cultural differences between Member States can be taken into account.

The question of the extent of the competences conferred is frequently referred to as the contrast between the "Europe of nations" and a "supranational Europe," or, put more simply, between the "sovereignists" and the "federalists." And the differences within the competences conferred are essentially related to unity and diversity, the degree of flexibility. What these two debates have in common is that neither can be resolved by an unequivocal acceptance or rejection of either proposition. Even the founding fathers wisely avoided the choice between a Europe of nations and a supranational Europe, leaving the debate essentially open, and relegating it to the future and to the interpretation of the Treaties. The Treaties regulate the extent of the competences conferred and the way in which they are to be exercised, and their intention is to establish a constantly renewing balance between the two approaches. Primarily in the political arena, the debate continues with varying degrees of intensity, all the more so because the Treaties in force refrain from definitively settling it. It would indeed be advisable to move away from the sharp either-or dichotomy and the historical and theoretical debates that this entails, and to come to different decisions on the division of competences in the various areas with a view to the objectives and realistic possibilities of integration. In any case, we must clearly see that the essence of the constitutional system of even the purest federations cannot arrogate the competences of its constituent entities, and that competences of the Member States must therefore be respected.

All the issues raised in the reinvigorated debate on the future of the European Union will decisively impact cooperation in Central Europe. The first and most important question is whether the original objective of a balance between the political, economic, and cultural dimensions can be achieved, as opposed to the current situation, which is characterized by the success and predominance of economic integration, the relegation of political objectives to a secondary role (viz. the feebleness of external action), and the marginalization of the cultural dimension, i.e., European identity based on historical and cultural heritage. The imbalance among the three dimensions has also affected the methods used, and the incremental technics of economic integration, reactiveness, gradualism, and functionalism have come to dominate all areas of integration. To top all this, centralization and unwarranted regulation have increased; indeed, a vicious circle of regulation without end has come into being, damaging the whole system.

It has been clear for several years however that the potential of this functionalist, technocratic method had been exhausted, and that not only was the balance to be restored but the methods were also to be renewed in order to move forward. And the method of achieving economic integration is not at all fit for attending to what is most important: European identity, European culture, our roots, our essence. There is no problem if we do not see eye to eye with one another on some elements of European identity or their order of importance. We recognize the importance of our ancient heritage and its Renaissance, but we also see Christian cathedrals and synagogues alongside Greek temples. We accept and profess the values of the Enlightenment; there is no Europe without freedom, equality, and fraternity. When we talk about human rights, we do not forget that the foundation of universal values was laid by the great world religions, and that the tenets of human freedom, dignity, responsibility, and equality were first developed by Christian philosophy. Together, these—alongside the respect for legal norms, rooted as they are in Roman law—form a common European cultural heritage and a united and diverse European identity, built by the past for the future. This is the cultural and anthropological basis of European integration, without the recognition and affirmation of which there can and will be no real union and no successful economic and political integration.

Moreover, no strengthening of European identity can be thought of without Central Europe and its contribution. This would require a better knowledge, understanding, and acceptance of this more turbulent part of Europe, its historical and cultural heritage, its experiences, achievements, and sensibilities. As well as a better understanding of the Central European soul, which is not happy to be called Eastern European—see, geography is returning to geopolitics together with geographical names—and is offended by being labelled post-communist. This Central Europe has not only embraced the tenets of liberty, equality, and fraternity but also has undertaken several revolutions and freedom fights to assert them.

If there are difficulties in the appreciation and recognition of Central Europe, this is a fault not only of a more fortunate "West" but also of we "Easterners." One of the most important tasks of the Visegrád Group and of Central European cooperation would therefore be to foster the dissemination and understanding of its unique values, the recognition and reception of its cultural and intellectual contribution. This is why it is important to take cognizance of the cultural and intellectual roots of our cooperation—this being also necessary in representing our special European—and Central European—identity at European level. At the same time, these foundations are also important for us because what we have to say about European integration also applies to our cooperation: without the cultural dimension and identity, there can be no successful economic and political integration.

Another important task for the future of European integration is to clarify, strengthen, and renew strategic objectives, to apply a new approach but remain within the current constitutional framework, i.e., without amending the Treaties. This also means respecting subsidiarity, national identity, including the constitutional identity and the competences of the political entities of integration, the Member States. The principle of non-arrogation of competences must also be applied in the European Union, regardless of the theoretical views on the nature of integration. The application of the "ever closer union" principle must be reviewed. This principle cannot be construed so as to imply that the provisions of the Treaties on the division of competences need not be fully respected. Competence creep violates the requirement of enforcing the rule of law at EU level and the very principles on which integration should be based. Ever closer union as a long-term principle of integration undoubtedly played an important role in driving the process forward, but it has now reached its political limits, and attempts to enforce it outside law are causing serious damage.

Central Europe has an important role to play in this change of mindset. The sense of European identity, of belonging to Europe and the European Union, is particularly strong, especially in Poland and Hungary, and is significantly stronger than the EU average. But, precisely for this reason, the sense of national identity is also much stronger in these countries (it is also much stronger in all Member States than the varying levels of European identity). This is why Central Europe, and within it the Visegrád Four, can authentically argue for the doctrine of national identity enshrined in the Founding Treaties and the constitutional identity deriving from it and its consistent application.

While visions of the renewal of integration and the future of Europe in general diverge, there is a consensus that one possible way forward is to identify areas where progress can and should be made under the given internal and external conditions. (This is the fourth of five scenarios in the White Paper the European Commission issued in spring 2017,[2] essentially meaning, in the brevity of its title: "Doing less more efficiently." The merit of these scenarios, moreover, is that they move away from the simplistic, binary logic of more Europe or less Europe, and try to outline more options. They can also build on each other, taking elements over from the others.) There is also a relatively broad consensus that, above all, this means external action, i.e., strengthening foreign policy, security, and defence policy, and enhancing the economic and commercial role of the European Union. The former is made imperative by major geopolitical changes, the emergence of new and old threats and risks, and the return of history, while the latter is made particularly opportune by changes in the conditions of international commercial policy. Oddly enough, one of the factors behind the changes in both the external security situation and the commercial-policy environment is the current marked retreat of the United States in the area of multilateral arms-control regimes and commercial agreements.

Demographically shrinking and ageing, losing economic space, Europe must comprehend that the peace dividend of integration does not cover external threats; true, we are no longer at war with each other, but we have failed to prepare for staving off external threats, and we are not strong enough. The world has become much more uncertain, unpredictable, and dangerous. From Russian imperial ambitions to Islamic fundamentalism, from China's global power aspirations to migration, which, caused either by nature or human activity, might reach unforeseeable proportions in the future, everything points to the need for Europe to undertake a greater part of its own security, substantially increase its defence capabilities, and allot many more resources to

---

[2] European Commission: WHITE PAPER ON THE FUTURE OF EUROPE. Reflections and scenarios for the EU27 by 2025 COM/2017/2025 final.

enhancing both its external and internal security. This requires a change in both mindset and organization. The recognition process is underway, the first steps have been taken (Permanent Structured Cooperation, PESCO), but further steps are needed in external and internal security equally.

If the world has become a more dangerous place, with increased risks for Europe, then Central Europe is exposed to even greater hazards, mainly due to geographical factors. This is why we say that not only history has returned but geography too, and unfortunately our region has become more exposed again, both because of the aforementioned ambitions of great powers and because of fundamentalism from the south and the imminent waves of mass immigration. We therefore have a particular interest in building a much stronger and more effective common foreign, security, and defence policy and in creating the necessary means to achieve this. We need to increase the contribution of Central Europe to strengthening our security and developing our defence capabilities, not only by supporting efforts to this end, but also by taking initiatives, as some examples have already shown in recent years. Stronger action in Central Europe must go hand in hand with stronger security and defence policy cooperation in Central Europe, essentially among the Visegrád Four.

The other important area where the European Union's external action needs to be stepped up is in the area of the international commercial system, regional trade agreements in particular. This process is well underway, with the European Union having concluded most of the agreements of the kind (we have more than fifty), but negotiations on other important agreements are now accelerating and promising a successful conclusion. Of these, the FTA with Japan is by far the most important in both economic and geopolitical terms. Opinion 2/15 of the European Court of Justice on the agreement with Singapore has in fact made it easier to conclude these agreements, but it is essential that this does not disregard the important interests of some Member States. The economies of Central Europe are the most open ones in the European Union, and it is in their vital interest to ensure the most favourable trade-policy conditions and to promote free, fair, and regulated trade. At the same time, we must pay particular attention to ensuring that our interests are not harmed in the negotiation of these agreements, all the more so as the qualified-majority decision in principle provides the legal opportunity to do so. So, on the one hand, we have an interest in further opening up to the world, in increasing Europe's economic and commercial (and thus geopolitical) role; on the other hand, we must be very firm in asserting the specific economic interests of the Central European Member States, both politically and legally.

Another priority is to strengthen and complete the single internal market. This includes the further development of the banking union, the capital markets union and the digital union, but the full implementation of the four freedoms as well as the reduction and gradual levelling out of differences in economic development are also indispensable to this.

This is the area where Central Europe needs to enforce its interests more assertively. The four freedoms are not fully applied, but the real challenge is that these principles are under serious attack, particularly in the area of the free movement of services. Suffice it to refer to the new EU legislation on posting staff abroad. The same applies to attempts by Member States to discriminate against workers from other Member States. On these issues, it is particularly important that not only the Visegrád Four, but all the Central European Member States act together and win over allies with similar interests. The same is true of cohesion policy, the most important instrument for levelling out differences in economic development. A substantial reduction in cohesion resources would undermine the possibility of creating a truly single internal market, and the same would be true if the instrument for closing the gap between levels of economic development were to be made dependent on politically motivated and discriminatory criteria that are alien to the economy. In the debate on the role and results of cohesion policy, we must make it clear that there is no real single market without this policy, and that the free movement of goods, services, capital, and labour makes it absolutely necessary to channel these resources to less developed regions, given the significant differences in development. For all the criticisms levelled at it, cohesion policy is far from being ineffective: the catching-up process is making progress, and cohesion policy is one of the factors behind the faster economic growth in the countries of Central Europe.

One of the most important questions for the further development of European integration in general, but for the Central European countries in particular, is whether a two- or multi-level union will emerge which would enable lasting, permanent (thus not temporary) divergences between individual Member States or groups of Member States, and which will put these divergences on a permanent legal and organizational footing. Would this lead to a Union of Unions, or would it be a way to fragment and dismantle the system that is currently unified despite the different speeds (euro or Schengen). The current divergences are mainly temporary ("speed"), and apply in a relatively narrow range under specific conditions.

The most important task for Central Europe in the current situation is to prevent a two- or multi-level integration structure. Attempts to do so have been underway for decades. The first impetus for such attempts came when the "threat" of "Eastern" enlargement, i.e., the reunification of Europe, appeared on television screens in the 1990s and the early golden age seemed to have waned, as a small table would not be enough to seat the Commissioners and the representatives of the Member State in the Council. Everything seemed simpler back then. Efforts to bring back the good old days have recently been revived. In the White Paper published by the Commission, the image of multi-level integration is presented in the third scenario, albeit in a relatively moderate form ("Those who want more do more"). If this version is but a form of enhanced cooperation already provided for by the Treaties and subject to appropriate conditions, it is not a cause for particular concern. Nor is speed difference to be worried about, as it is still part of the legal regulation and the reality of the integration process. A degree of flexibility and of differentiation is necessary because of the considerable differences between Member States and the need to move on. Fragmentation is a serious risk however, the toxic effects of which could jeopardize integration as a whole. Visegrád and the countries of Central Europe cannot accept any dividing line that would justify a European Union based on different levels. The argument in our favour is that such a structure would not even be viable, there is no single dividing line within the European Union—geographical, historical, economic, political, or cultural—that would undergird it and last forever.

The cooperation and political action of the Visegrád Four can by no means provide a basis for creating permanent dividing lines within the European Union. Like other regional cooperations (Benelux, Nordic countries, Baltic countries), Visegrád is based on genuine historical, geographical, economic, and security policy factors but does not reinforce divisions; on the contrary, it is a building block for cooperation among all Member States. This quarter of a century of cooperation, which has varied in intensity but has proved lasting and successful, also plays an important role in driving forward the process of European integration. Visegrád is therefore needed by the European Union as a whole, and further strengthening cooperation is meant not to divide Member States but to enable the successful continuation and renewal of integration. To see Visegrád and Central European cooperation in general as a factor of East–West division is just as serious a mistake as to see the V4 position on immigration as the only important cohesive element of that cooperation.

In the way Central European identity is part and parcel of European identity, a more intense version of it, so the Visegrád and Central European co-operation is an inseparable part of the European Union. Central Europe is bound to the European Union by its history, geographical location, economic, geopolitical, and security interests, and an independent Central European integration cannot and will never be an alternative. Visegrád must not be allowed to stand in the way of the mainstream of European integration, as it is an indispensable component of it. There is no Central Europe outside Europe, and there is no Europe without Central Europe. Attempts at division and political efforts to create multi-level integration threaten the full application of this obvious premise.

Elemér Hantos was therefore right not to accept the contrasting of Central European and pan-European or even economic and political integration, and to interpret the relationship between the two as a matter of the chronological order of their realization. Central Europe was excluded by history and geopolitics from the process of European integration for a few decades, but reunification took place after the *annus mirabilis*, somewhat belatedly. It would be a historical mistake to carve up a reunited Europe again with new dividing lines based on false theories.

Cooperation among the Visegrád Four is therefore part of the whole, an important and indispensable part of European integration. It is built on enduring values and interests, but it has in no way exhausted its potential. Nor can we claim that it has solved all the problems of our region, all the inherited disagreements, the possible disputes and tensions. Infrastructural development is very important, building railways, motorways, oil and gas pipelines, bridges, but virtual, intellectual bridges based on shared values and a sense of belonging are even more important. We have a lot to do, but we are on the right track.

Different Perspectives – Common Interests

College of Visegrád, Stratégiai Tanulmányok Intézete [Strategic Studies Institute], 28–29 November 2019, NKE, Budapest

Let me welcome all of you, I really appreciate the trouble you all have taken to come to Budapest, especially in this November weather. Next time I will suggest organising such meetings either in May or in October. However, it is timely. I understand that the main purpose of this conference, after all, is to raise the public awareness of Visegrád, which is a huge task. We did not really succeed in doing that during the past now more than twenty-five years. There are still many false perceptions, which of course we try to dispel, but it is not easy. On the other hand, the purpose of this meeting is also to discuss the present and the future; how can we adapt to the new situation, and where do we see the main tasks and responsibilities of the Visegrád Four? Maybe on a more general level of Central Europe within a European, transatlantic and global context.

Now let me say one or two words about history. I will not start it in 1335; we will have an interesting presentation later today about the historic background, which is very relevant even now. I might come back to this a little bit when I talk about one of the main challenges we are now confronting. But I will limit myself to the last three decades, or at least to the time of the idea of doing something or creating something in a unique historic situation, which was at and right after the time of the huge changes in this part of the world. There were essentially two paths in front of the Central-, or Eastern-

Central, or Central-Eastern European countries. (As we know, even the names are somewhat hazy here.) One was—to put it bluntly—just to continue the kind of confrontation, the kind of rivalry that was an old game we had been playing for centuries. Whether these were dynasties or sovereign countries or parts of some different larger political units, this kind of jealousy and rivalry had always been there. And also of course, some conflicts.

The second way was to get rid of this negative side of history and to start a relatively new kind of cooperation that we call "cooperation culture" instead of the "confrontation culture." The cooperation culture, of course, also had very deep roots. We should not forget about that. Not just through a long range of centuries, but also, and more importantly in the last forty-five years, which we call communism. Because all through these more than four decades a sense of solidarity developed progressively, gradually among our nations – and I deliberately use the word "nation." As I said, the solidarity was progressively developed. It was fairly weak at the beginning but was progressively strengthened by a list of all the uprisings in Berlin, Poznań, Budapest (which was in fact the whole of Hungary, because the Hungarian revolution and freedom fight extended to the whole country), then Prague, Czechoslovakia, Ursus, the Lenin Shipyard, Poland, and so on.

All through these developments, the solidarity rooted in the common aspiration for freedom and national independence increased and deepened. At the beginning there was a little bit of silence, even mutual reproaches on the part of Hungarian intellectuals and Czech intellectuals, for instance, about the behaviour of the other side at the time of their national uprisings. But it progressively diminished, and we realized—I still recall the conversations which we had as students many years ago—that we only have a chance to do something against the Soviet Empire if we stick together and do something together. Otherwise, there is no chance. Because if we do it separately—Hungarians, Czechs, Slovaks, Poles, whoever—it will never work. But once we get together, it might change. How did it happen? I don't want to get into the details, but clearly, there was a historic opportunity, which was created by the global developments as well. I would like to underline very firmly that the most important development took place here in Central Europe. First and foremost, Poland. Therefore, we should never forget it. Other countries of course followed in different ways; Hungarians were experimenting with reforms, whether it worked or not, that's a different story; but all in all, the Central-European role in the fundamental global geopolitical change played an indispensable role.

One of the false perceptions, which I referred to briefly before, is that this Visegrád cooperation was only established because these countries wanted to establish a scheme of cooperation so that they could get into the so-called Euro-Atlantic structures, such as the European Community and NATO, faster and more easily. There were, of course external factors as well, we cannot deny it. Among these external factors there was an imminent task, which was to dismantle the existing structures, which were the CMEA and the Warsaw Pact. First and foremost, we had to get out of those structures. As it turned out, we managed to abolish, to terminate them without any successor organization. Here I feel obliged to mention the name of the Hungarian prime minister at that time, József Antall, who played a key role, especially regarding the termination of the Warsaw Pact without a successor organization. There was a famous meeting in Moscow at which Antall read out a text which was not fully prepared and agreed upon, but for whatever reasons—it is not yet fully clear—Gorbachev said "Хорошо," and with that it was settled. That was the first external factor, which was the most urgent and important.

On the other hand, there was the gradually developing sense of solidarity, based on which a kind of mutual trust was emerging. Behind the emerging trust and solidarity there was a fundamental cultural, historic factor, a distinctive cultural legacy, which we tried to define from time to time and which we can now safely call Central-European identity, a Central-European collective identity. I cannot give you a perfect definition of what it is; first of all, we cannot even give a geographic definition of Central Europe. We also have another cooperation scheme called the Central-European Initiative, where we now have eighteen members, so it is not easy to define where the geographic borders of Central Europe are located. It is not even a strictly necessary geopolitical concept, although there are geopolitical interests which are common in the region. The real and the essential basis is culture. As it is sometimes said, "It is always culture that matters."

We are Central Europeans. What does this mean? It means, first and foremost, that we are Europeans. It is a key element; we are all Europeans. It is not a question of aspirations; it is also a question of responsibility. At the same time, we have a distinctive cultural and historic legacy, and we do have a kind of identity. Many years ago, my definition was that Central Europe is primarily part of Europe. Secondly, it means that it is a denser, a more intensive, a more diverse Europe—a stronger diversity of languages, of religions. Do not forget that in Central Europe even the crosses have different shapes in different communities. In Centra -Europe, we used to have—before the Holocaust—the highest number of synagogues per capita. So diversity was running very high, and of course, we had our own sensitivities based on historic reasons. We had many complexes—in most cases an inferiority complex, which we are still living with in a way. To offset the inferiority complexes, we developed a superiority complex, which is a natural consequence of or reaction to an inferiority complex. We are melancholic, but we also have a highly developed sense of humour, creativity, ingenuity. All these can be discussed; some people say that we also have a sense of humour like that of the British, for example. We are distinctive. I think that was the basic reason for having the sense of belonging to something which we could share. I think without that the Visegrád cooperation could not have been established.

There were of course basic economic interests; perhaps trade is the best example. At the time when the change came, trade and economic ties in general—of course investment did not exist in those days—were limited. Again, there is a general perception that these countries were intensively trading with each other within the framework of COMECON. However, in reality, the trade with each other was fairly modest. At the same time, they all traded a lot with the Soviet Union. They did not even have the necessary mechanism to trade with each other; they used bilateral clearing accounts, and just because they had a sense of humour, they called the bilateral clearing units transferable rubles, because they were neither transferable nor rubles. Some of us already were members of GATT, so we adopted the universal, general rules. Did we have to introduce tariffs and all other kinds of barriers? Yes, we had to, because we were obliged by the international framework we joined. Then came the idea "why don't we make a free trade agreement?" If we cannot do it immediately, we will do it by sitting down and negotiating with each other; it will take some time, but we can do it. Of course, we will fully apply the respective articles of GATT, like Art. 24. And we did it; we negotiated and concluded the Central European Free Trade Agreement (CEFTA). It turned out to be not only successful but also attractive, because others also wanted to and did join it. If you look back at the trade figures of those years, you will find that trade among our countries increased. That was the first success. At the same time, basic geopolitical considerations and objectives also brought us together.

Now, in short, the original objectives of the V4 cooperation were attained. The famous reconciliation—as it is often referred to between France and Germany—worked in a Central European context. We should never forget that reconciliation, in a political and cultural sense as well, is not a one-off exercise, it is a permanent exercise. It is a permanent job; differences, small conflicts might always emerge. So we have to settle them, we have to tackle them. But the framework is there; any kind of bilateral dispute or conflict can be tackled and resolved in those three or four regional frameworks with a better result, without resorting to anybody outside. This was another basic consideration. Until then, all through the centuries, we were trying to find the support of external Big Brothers. We were running to Vienna, we were running to Berlin, we were running to Paris and some people were running to Moscow. Let us stop it. We were always grateful for advice, but please, let us settle our own problems ourselves! That basic policy is still valid.

Two of the basic external objectives were therefore attained, dismantling the existing eastern structures and joining the western ones. When we joined the European Union, some people raised the idea that the V4 may be over. (By the way, CEFTA was really over, at least for those who joined the EU, because the EU was the new structure, of course, which entered into force.) Then the answer immediately came that no, the V4 is here, and it is here to stay. The V4 will be at least as relevant and real in the upcoming decades as it has been until now because we will have to represent common interests, primarily within the European Union and also in the other transatlantic structures. Because of our historic, geographic, cultural, economic background, we have common interests, as has been best demonstrated in the last couple of years.

When we had the 10th, 15th, 20th, then the 25th anniversaries for the V4, we always underlined with force and determination that we were going to continue. Why? Because we had confirmed that the results were there. Just take the European Union. The areas of cooperation are unlimited. Just to tell you one or two: the best test, the MFF, the multiannual financial framework, is here. It will be an extremely important issue for each of our countries. What will be the final outcome? Until now, the final outcome for our countries has not been bad. But this time we are running the risk that the overall level of financial support will go down by 15 and 24 percent, as an average for our region. For Hungary, according to the present figures, the cutback will be 24 percent. So there will be a joint fight, even if we all know that we also have national interests, but until now, the common interest has always prevailed, despite the existing specific national considerations and interests.

The money is no doubt a key question, whether it is the cohesion fund, or whether it is regarding agriculture. As regards agriculture, there are also some slight differences. Some countries are more interested than others, but the overall interest is to maintain and to continue these policies. Then we have the single market, which is not yet complete. Especially in those areas which are most important for us, for instance, the area of services. We all know the story which is now going around about the "posted workers." This is in an ongoing debate, and we—the V4 and Central Europeans—represent the same interests. Then we have the enlargement, which is the most recent example. We are all interested in the continuation of the enlargement process. We are also very much interested in a successful neighbourhood policy, especially the Eastern neighbourhood policy because our security is directly concerned. We are all interested in an open trade policy; we are all interested in negotiating and making free trade agreements, as we have to be free traders given that we all have open economies exporting 85 or 90 percent of our GDP. So we need markets, we need foreign resources, and that, again, is a common point. Of course, we can go on; there are other important things like defence. We are all interested in a stronger defence; that is why we set up the V4 - EU battle group together. We are all interested in maintaining Schengen, and we need to have strong and secure borders. We need to have a functioning Schengen, which cannot exist without strong and protected external borders. And that brings us to the question of migration, where we also have common stands. That might create some disputes with some other countries, but I think more and more people understand that without strong and secure borders we cannot maintain the "acquis," the achievements we have attained until now. So all these are common interests, and the list goes on.

Then comes the question: What is to be done in the future? We have a couple of major challenges. One is no doubt that we are speaking of Central-European identity, Central-European geographical and economic interests, but we are the V4. V4 and Central Europe in whatever sense you take Central Europe, are not identical. We can say that we are the centre of gravity of Central Europe. We have a kind of centrality in this part of Europe. But we are not the same as Central Europe. That of course brings us to the dilemma of the enlargement of V4. This is a very old topic. Some countries wanted to join, and the usual answer has been until now that the problem is that we are not a formal organization, we do not even have an institutional structure. V4 is a brand, a flexible, somewhat informal dialogue and cooperation, which we cannot expand like the European Union or any other organization. But a solution still needs to be found. One of the things we suggested a couple of years ago was that we should develop a closer circle within the well-known V4+ structure. V4+ means anyone—now almost fifty countries have been covered by V4+, from Japan to India, from Turkey to Egypt. This demonstrates the geopolitical and economic importance of V4, as so many countries wanted and still want to talk to us and sit down with us. But this is a larger circle, practically the whole world, because we are open, we are ready to sit down with everyone. But at the same time, we should design a special structure, a special circle for those who cannot be members of the V4. Because V4 is V4. But of course, those with whom we could and should develop very special cooperation—those are our close neighbours like Slovenia, Croatia, Romania, Austria. Other schemes of cooperation have also been developed, and we have a diversity of cooperation forms, which may be called "Europe Centrale à géométrie variable." However, we also say that Visegrád has to be maintained as it is, and we have to develop cooperation schemes with all the others. This is something, which we have to look after, and have to resolve somehow. Clearly, we cannot say that we are the only and exclusive cooperation in Central Europe.

We have a large number of tasks for the future. An interesting report was prepared three years ago at the time of the 25th anniversary of V4, by eight so called Eminent Persons, two from each of the four countries. In this report, there are interesting suggestions and propositions. Let me mention just one: I was talking about the free trade agreement CEFTA, about the results, the achievements. But now—even if we are all part of the EU and we enjoy the single market—interestingly trade is still not sufficiently developed among our countries. We talk a lot about infrastructure, high-speed railway, and pipelines—it is an ongoing permanent subject, but we should do much more in this area. As far as our level of economic development is concerned, we all have a similar challenge, which is the so called "middle income trap." We survived the global financial crisis very well, especially Poland, which was the single European country that did not stop growing, though apparently these possibilities of further growth seem to be narrowing. What we should do is to increase, multiply not only trade but also capital movements between our countries. We should bring our somewhat isolated capital markets closer to one another; we should develop equity financing on a cross-border level.

These are all extremely important challenges. We must reach a higher place on the so-called "value chains" or "supply chains" which now decide everything. Our British friends will learn how important supply chains are in a couple of years. So we have to develop this, and we have to think about new schemes, all within the EU framework. We do not want to develop a legal or institutional structure, but still we have to do something in order to increase our internal connections and communication. And all this should be done in a bottom-up way. In a way, this is being done, and this is the line that we should follow. My examples refer to trade and economic relations in general, but the same applies to culture. We established the famous Visegrád Fund, we increased its resources—not very significantly, but still it was a good beginning. Hopefully, we will try to increase it in the future—all kinds of cultural cooperation and scholarships and many other things. We should do much more. We should benefit much more from that historic legacy upon which—as we have seen—our cooperation is based.

The final conclusion is that Visegrád is here to stay. And if we really want to continue and develop it further we need a stronger bottom-up approach—in investments, in economic relations, in every possible area, including of course think-tanks, universities, people who think, discuss, propose, invent and create, which—as I understand—is the purpose of this conference. So welcome again, and I wish you a fruitful and successful discussion.

Thank you for your attention.

Presentation on the Role of Law and Identity in European Integration

Delivered at the Fourteenth Hungarian Lawyers' Conference at Balatonalmádi, 5 October 2018.[1]

Ladies and gentlemen, dear colleagues, welcome to you all!

First of all, I must apologize, because what I am going to talk about is not quite the same as what is in the title. Six years ago, in this same hotel, perhaps in the same room, I spoke about the relationship between European law and Hungarian law, with special regard to constitutional identity. This was not a new concept even at the time, yet it was already apparent that the phenomenon observable both in European practice and in Hungary would be of particular importance in the years to come. Now, I was asked to speak again about the relationship between European law and Hungarian law. I indicated that I had already spoken about this once, and I would not be keen on repeating what I had said. True enough, though, there have been several developments in the six years that have gone by since. So, I gave it a thought whether I should rehash my earlier discussion or not. I decided that I would rather not, if only because the upcoming lecture or lectures would occasion bringing it up.

Let me outline the five questions I intend to talk about. First, I wish to review what has happened over the last six years, briefly touching on develop-

---

[1] First published in Benisné Győrffy, Ilona (ed.), *XIV. Magyar Jogászgyűlés Kiadványa*, Budapest: Magyar Jogász Egylet, 2018.

ments at home and detailing the main changes in the European context. For important things have occurred there too, perhaps not primarily in the context of European law and constitutional identity but in the relationship between international law and European law, and these developments also directly affect the subject of my narrower focus, namely the relationship between European law and national laws, including constitutional identity. The second question I wish to dwell on is the role of law in European integration, particularly in its different economic, political, and cultural dimensions. As a matter of fact, the latter is the "identity" indicated in the title.

The third topic is the nature of European law and its place in an increasingly insipid normative hierarchy. This topic will occasion a few words about the relationships between international law, European law, and national laws. In this context, I shall have to broach the direct effect of international law, the limits that European law imposes on international law, and the way in which these transpire in the relationship between European law and national laws, constitutional identity in particular, and therefore the limits that national law and national constitutions impose on the unrestricted enforcement of European law. My penultimate topic will be how this issue arises in a specific area, the field of international economic relations and, within that, in the area of investment protection. Currently, this is the hottest topic, the subject of the most debate, numerous studies and conferences, the sharpest exchanges, and the most critical comments on the case-law of the European Court of Justice, which I would not dare to quote in this forum. In any case, this is the most thrilling subject at the moment, both from a theoretical and a practical point of view, and the debate around it is being played out in ongoing major international investment disputes, in some of which the defendant or the plaintiff is Hungarian.

Finally, I shall treat the consequences of this theoretical and practical debate and ask what the future has in store. It is not easy to tell, of course, but some predictions can be made. There is much debate over the consequences, many saying and writing that the current process may have adverse consequences the universal rule of law and on the international movement of capital, even the movement of capital between Member States. I mentioned how a certain normative hierarchy—which many now preferring to call a heterarchy—affects the rule of law, legal security, and the predictability of the outcome of legal disputes. This is an important area. I shall also analyze the impact and the consequences of these disputes and criticisms on the European integration institutions, the European Court of Justice in particular.

As regards the very first question, we know the ruling of the Constitutional Court on constitutional identity and the text of the amendment to the Constitution, the Fundamental Law. I need not really go into this, as it will perhaps be brought up by the next lecture or lectures. In any event, the issue has been tabled, and European constitutional courts are following the line detailed here six years ago, namely that they are imposing limits to the absolute primacy of European law by way of constitutional court rulings and invoking Article 4(2) of the Treaty, which mentions national identity. However, we know very well that actually means not the identity of the nation in the cultural sense but the constitutional identity deriving from the sovereignty of the State. The text explicitly highlights the issue of the constitutional and political establishment. It is thus clear that we are dealing here with a public-law barrier linked to the state. Ultimately, it derives from the sovereignty of the state, particularly as the principle of conferral of competences has been enshrined at least three times in the Treaties since Lisbon. And this conferral naturally derives from the sovereignty of the Member States.

As far as European developments are concerned, the autonomy of European law is increasingly undergirded by the rulings and opinions of the European Court of Justice. Where the exact limits of this autonomy are and will be, we cannot tell, not least because these limits seem to be shifting; they sometimes depend on decisions, and the intended outcome determines them. So, it is difficult to define the actual doctrine, its guiding principle. European case-law not being bound by precedents, we cannot say exactly what effect a previous decision will have on the next one. We might have inklings, and I shall perhaps risk some predictions concerning investment protection, but it goes without saying, with no certainty.

The second theme is a familiar one, but it is necessary in order to understand the essence of the dilemma. European integration was brought about by law, the edifice was erected by international law, and law developed and built it further. On the one hand, even primary law has often been amended, think of the amendments to the Founding Treaties, including the Accession Treaties, because enlargement as such leads to amendment. Secondary law develops organically and continuously, and this is one of the main features of the European integration process, especially the economic part, where law is partly reactive and partly a driver of further development, and, as an instrument, it plays a decisive role in building European integration. As a matter of course, the case law of the European Court of Justice also has a decisive impact on the process. The role of law is different in the three main dimensions of European integration. As an instrument, it has a decisive role in economic integration. The single market requires permanent law-making, without which it would not be able to function. But the situation is similar in many other areas. The moment something needs to be reformed, the question immediately arises what draft legislation the European Commission should prepare. The two words that we have heard most often in the process of European integration over the last sixty years are *crisis* and *reform*. We have crises, and we always respond to them with some kind of reform, and we would not be able to manage them without law. Another important area of integration is the political dimension. Here, law plays a considerably lesser role. Political decisions are taken; in the area of common foreign, security, and defence policy there are essentially no binding legal acts that can be challenged in court. In this area, decisions being essentially political, law has but a complementary or formal role at most.

The third dimension is culture, the least developed area of integration. Law does not play a significant role here either. Moreover, the underdevelopment of the cultural dimension is closely linked to issues of community identity. By debate, dialogue, and the exchange of ideas, the first task would be to clarify the main content of European identity. The emphases are probably placed elsewhere in, say, today's Paris and Budapest. So, the picture here is varied, but if we agree—and it seems we now do—that there is a community identity, a European identity, which is obviously secondary to national identity, then there would be no obstacle to developing the essential content of this European identity.

One difference between the three dimensions is thus that law plays a very different role in each, and another difference is that the degree of success they achieve is likewise different. Economic integration, I continue to maintain, is an amazing success. It is unprecedented in a thousand and many hundred years in the history of Europe. In this success, law as a technique, as a tool, and as a conceptual system has played a decisive role. Political integration is often said to be half success, because though it can undoubtedly boast elements of success, it obviously lags far behind the economy. It is in foreign-, security-, and defence policy that we are most falling behind and are now starting to gear up slowly, which also means strengthening the political dimension. Above all, it must be seen that without a stronger cultural dimension and identity—without clarifying the concept of European identity—we cannot move the economic process forward, even with the most sophisticated legal instruments. This is what we now have to admit; and many people are admitting it. Where one finds the solution is another matter, but we all agree we cannot move the economic process forward using the classic reactive, functional, incremental, and organic techniques, and we need something new.

Thus, in all three areas, law as an instrument has played, and continues to play a crucial role, yet crucial at varying degrees. There is nothing wrong with this. Law is a very important tool for achieving socio-political, economic or other policy objectives. At the end of the 1980s, I heard Tamás Sárközy, the current president of the Hungarian Lawyers Association, say, when the debate was on whether we could use law as a tool to prepare major socio-economic changes, that yes, we must use law for this purpose, but we must respect the conceptual system and structure of law, and the only way we can be successful in using it as a tool is by respecting its structure and conceptual system. If we do not respect it, the instrument will be dysfunctional, and we will not achieve the intended result. We must therefore use the law to achieve the main objectives of European integration, but we must do so in full respect of the structure and conceptual system of law, broadly, the fundamental principles of the rule of law.

Simultaneously, law is not only a tool in the integration process but also an important element of the cultural dimension, European identity. It is therefore not only a tool but also a value in itself. It is not by chance that we say that there are three main elements of European identity: the Acropolis, our ancient heritage, Golgotha, our Judeo-Christian heritage, and Roman law, the legal culture based on norms. Being a normative approach, the resolution of socio-economic conflicts within the framework of legal provisions, law—broadly assuming a horizontal relationship between the parties—is therefore central to European identity. This is what makes us European. So, while law is a tool, it is also an intrinsic value in the whole process, and, for that reason alone, we cannot give up the proper use of this tool.

The next subject is the relationship between the three levels, including international law, European law, and national laws, and the relationship between the first two levels. For decades, scores of researchers have been working on this theme, which, in addition to its stimulating and fascinating theoretical elements, also has a very important practical impact. The first question is this: Is European law international law or not? We have debated this here at home. From the Hungarian legislator's point of view, secondary law is not international law, because Article E of the Fundamental Law clearly states that the law of the European Union lays down generally binding rules of conduct, whereas international law must be made part of the Hungarian legal system, except for, of course, *jus cogens*, the generally binding rules. European law itself is born of, created by international law, and primary law is itself international law, so the Founding Treaties are part of international law. The European Union is also an international legal entity, it has legal personality, it is subject to international law, bound by the norms of international law, and also liable to international law. Nor is it disputed that the European Union is not only a subject of international law but also a major actor of international law, as it creates a substantial part of it, its Founding Treaties being incorporated into an otherwise increasingly plural and fragmented international legal system and a set of its established institutions eventually being taken over by global and international regulation.

European law therefore has a continuous formative role, which is why we say that European law is in some ways a laboratory of the development of global law. However, there are also a number of unresolved issues. In its doctrinal purity, the nature of European law is not clear as long as the nature of European integration, of the European Union, is not clear. We do not know whether the European Union is an international organization or a quasi-federal state. What we do know is that it is neither; yet it is an organization *sui generis*. It is obviously unlike any other international organization, but it is certainly not a federal state, not even a confederation. Perhaps that is what the phrase "ever closer union" is intended to imply, but it is precisely this turn of phrase that is coming in for increasing criticism. It is not clear, therefore, whether European law is the law of a (semi-) federal state or whether it is a system of norms created by an international organization which blend with or fit into international law.

From the point of view of European law, the most important thesis is the autonomy of European law. The European Union is a constitutional edifice; European law is based on values, it has principles and a comprehensive and coherent set of norms. As a constitutional system, it has its own autonomy, which it defends against everyone. It protects it everywhere by way of infringement procedures, because the European legal system responds with infringement procedures, where it feels that it has been infringed in some way by any of its Member States. But European law also seeks to defend its identity, which it calls its autonomy with respect to international law. Again, there is no clear definition of autonomy. It includes various substantive elements, but its exact framework and scope are undefined.

International law is enforced or manifest in European law in three ways. First, it has direct effect within a certain scope and under certain conditions. Until 2008, the thesis was that the presumption of the direct effect of international law could be refuted, and was refuted in some cases, but direct effect remained the main rule. There was one important exception, incidentally, the area of international commercial regulation, namely GATT/WTO, where international regulations have never had, and still do not have, direct effect. But since 2008, there has been a significant shift in emphasis, as a result of which the concept of autonomy has been substantially strengthened, and the direct effect of international law has increasingly been subjected to limitations. Though there is a consolation prize: if there is no direct effect, we construe the rules of European law in harmony and consistently with international law. In the absence of this, there remains a third option: borrowing and using the basic concepts of international law.

These, then, are the three ways international affects European law. The really interesting issue is the first one, direct effect, which tends to gradually diminish. There was however one case where, oddly enough, the customary international law norm not only did not regress but gained ground—indeed, it reversed the process. This was a case in which Hungary was the plaintiff and Slovakia the defendant, and President László Sólyom's failed trip to Slovakia was the subject of the lawsuit. Here, the European Court of Justice ruled exactly the opposite way it had done before in a long series of judgments, and found that, although European law governs, it does not always apply and not to everyone. One of the four fundamental freedoms, the principle of free movement of persons, does not apply to a head of state. The decision was sharply criticized in the literature, and we still do not know how far the exception allegedly created by customary international law extends to the highest dignitaries, and, thus, ultimately, who is excluded from the circle of persons enjoying the fundamental freedom. Case law is therefore changing, and the question arises whether there is a settled doctrine, or a decision is adapted to the result intended.

As a "last plea," let me say a few words about investment protection, a topic much discussed these days. In short, the essence of the matter is that in its preliminary ruling in the Achmea case, the European Court of Justice ruled that arbitration clauses are invalid in bilateral investment protection agreements between Member States. The ruling is correct and well founded. That is not the problem, it is that the reasoning is imprecise and indeterminate, and therefore it is not possible to know whether the reasons given in the judgment, which are otherwise set out in a logical system, are to be applied to arbitration clauses in other investment protection agreements or not. In the Energy Charter, for example, the contracting parties are the Member States, but the European Union as a subject of international law is also a contracting party, and so are a number of countries that are not members of the European Union. The question arises whether the Energy Charter is also governed by the invalidity of an arbitration clause between two Member States. Recently, in a very notable arbitration case (Vattenfall v. Germany), three wise arbitrators ruled that the Achmea doctrine, i.e., the invalidity of the arbitration clause, does not apply to the Energy Charter. Simultaneously, the European Commission stated in a Communication that the Achmea judgment also applies to the Energy Charter. This is where we are now. In two cases, the arbitrators announced that they did not consider the ECJ ruling to be binding, that they would continue to hear the case, rejected the jurisdictional challenge, and would rule on the merits. This decision will, of course, not be enforceable in the European Union.

Beyond the theoretical debate, there are thus important practical issues and implications. One of the consequences may be that the parties will try to avoid the territory of the European Union, particularly as regards the seat of arbitration. The possibilities are numerous, including Switzerland, Singapore, New York, and London after 30 March of course. The other consequence may be that the parties avoid choosing the law of an EU Member State as the governing law. The third consequence, and a practising lawyer actually would start with this, is that the arbitral award cannot be enforced in the European Union. The property to be seized must therefore be sought and located outside the territory of the European Union. Theoretical tenets thus boil down to concrete, practical issues, and businesses are already reacting to them in practice. We have a fundamental interest in the international movement of capital, but if the European Union is at a disadvantage in this respect, it could have negative economic consequences. It is therefore not at all certain that a positive process has been set in motion. But a judgment in the CETA case is forthcoming, and the European Court of Justice will hopefully provide a more precise and more determinate reasoning, but what exactly the doctrine will be is difficult to say.

Six years ago, I said, on the issue of constitutional identity, that we should listen to each other, engage in dialogue, and take into account what is particularly important for the other side, for example, a Member State. There is also self-restraint in the world, because if a forum wants to maximally enforce its own position, it will inevitably harm the other one, and the other one will respond. This is not a fitting approach for international and European cooperation. We must engage in dialogue not only over judgments but also through science. Above all, what practice needs is predictability, greater certainty, legal certainty created by a more stable judicial practice.

Thank you very much for your attention.

Keynote Address to the Conference on the 70ᵗʰ anniversary of the foundation of the Council of Europe

Conference on the 70ᵗʰ Anniversary of the Foundation of the Council of Europe, 21 November 2019. Budapest European Youth Centre[1]

There is an old debate about what came first in the age of discovery, the gun, the warship, and the flag carried by the warship, or the merchant, carrying the glass beads and the firewater and exchanging those for other goods. In other words, was the political and the military power, the state and its embodiment, the flag, first, or was it trade, was it the economy? This debate has not been decided to this day, because there were times when the merchant was there first, there were times when it was the warship, and there were times when both arrived at the same time, for the sake of security. However, we usually speak less about a third player, although it is actually not at all impossible that someone preceded the other two. This was the missionary, who had no glass beads, no firewater, and no cannon. He was carrying Holy Scripture. We may say that he was carrying the "Bible."

This triple interconnection is still a given in the world, in the history of mankind, in geopolitics, everywhere. The debate may continue in our times —no longer about which appeared on that particular island first, but about which is the more important. Is it the economy? We know the philosophical stream which considered the economy to be the key factor, determining all other areas. Or is it possibly the political power with military might behind

---

[1] Published as: "70 Years in Europe," Institute for Foreign Affairs and Trade, Budapest 2020.

it? Is it the number of military divisions, the number of nuclear warheads and carriers? When it was raised to Stalin that the Vatican would not be pleased with his anti-church policy in Central- and Eastern Europe, he replied by asking how many tank divisions the Vatican had. Thus, the issue was settled. It is a different question now that the Soviet Union ceased to exist long ago, while the Vatican is still around. Undoubtedly the Vatican has its own challenges to address, but it is nevertheless a longer-term and deeper story.

In Europe after the Second World War all three key factors appear. There is an economic approach saying that the shattered European economies should be brought closer together and that at least the economic and trade barriers between them should gradually be removed. The story is well-known: we started with coal and steel, which were at that time the foundations of industry as a whole, not to mention that it did no harm to subject the coal and steel industries of certain countries to more serious scrutiny before they manufactured too many tanks and airplanes. Therefore, an economic integration is launched, and the move towards the unification of the flag also begins, even to the extent of elaborating the idea of a European defense community, together with that of a European political community. It is another story that these two communities are eventually rejected in the French National Assembly, even though they were originally French initiatives.

But something else also happens, which is our subject today. The Council of Europe is established. It is immediately clear that the Council of Europe has not a single tank division. It does not make plans to enter this territory either. It also comes to light that, unlike the EU, the Council of Europe does not have a cohesion fund to enable it to subsidize the less developed economies with several billions of euros. Nor is it in a position to support the agricultural sector with enormous subsidies. This represents something deeper; it is a much more important matter. Its mission is to interpret that aforementioned scripture of the missionary and to enforce it, predominantly with the instruments of law.

The three main areas the Council of Europe has to look after are democracy, rule of law, and human rights. These three areas are prerequisites for one another, and none can exist in the absence of the others. As far as the interpretation and the implementation are concerned, this is not a simple matter. Interpreting and enforcing the scripture is a difficult and dangerous task, which requires taking a lot of responsibility. When interpreting the scripture and declaring it as law, one must pay attention to a lot of things, for example to keeping the external, the political aspects at a distance. It did not always work out that way. Possibly, it does not always work out that way nowadays either.

Now we are celebrating the 70th anniversary, and we were celebrating the 50th anniversary twenty years ago, which was a very special occasion for us: Hungary had been member of the Council for almost ten years, so we also celebrated a 10th anniversary. Since joining the Council, Hungary has very intensively taken part in its work, and the Hungarian contributions are significant. We should never lose sight of the fact that for us at present and in the future, the rights of national minorities are the most important ones. We shall never give them up, and we can evaluate the Council and its various institutions primarily in the light of how they enforce the rights of national minorities. We do not only mean individual rights, but also the rights of national communities, we mean collective rights. This is something we will never relinquish, and if we see that in any other country these rights, whether linguistic or educational, are not granted, we will voice this in the most decisive way.

This is the point in my speech when I return to its starting point. It is a fact that the warship exists, there is security and defense policy and there is economic policy. The various international organizations are entrusted with the task of looking after these separable fields. But we should not forget that the scripture applies to all of these. It applies to the European economic and political integration, it applies to the defense and security policy organizations, and it applies to NATO, too. That specific scripture which created the Council of Europe is its foundation, and the values, principles, and norms included in it must manifest themselves in all the other organizations.

The Schuman Declaration – Seventy Years Ago and Now

Intended to be delivered at the international conference on the occasion of the seventieth anniversary of the Schuman Declaration on 11 May 2020, but cancelled due the pandemic.[1]

I have devoted three essays to European integration,[2] and they understandably cover only a scant twenty-five years of the seven decades since the Schuman Declaration. Yet the fundamental issues and dilemmas were essentially the same or similar, and indeed remain so today. Of course, the world is changing constantly and rapidly, and this is also true of European integration. Changes sometimes accelerate, and, in extreme situations, such as the current pandemic, we repeat the wise, if not very original, observation that the world will never be the same again. It is true; the world is never the same as it was the day before, and it is also true that extraordinary events and shocks not only speed up change but also give new direction to processes and can slow down or even stop certain processes that were already underway and gaining pace. The Covid-19 epidemic, for example, will slow down globalization, particularly in the economy. However, this slowdown was already un-

---

1 Published in *Európai Tükör*, volume 23 (2020), number 2, issue 2, 117–128.
2 Martonyi, János, "A magyar nemzet sorsa és az európai fejlődés" (The Fate of the Hungarian Nation and European Progress), in *Európa, nemzet, jogállam*. Budapest: Magyar Szemle – Európai Utas. 1998, 125–132; idem., "Hogyan tovább, Európa?" (What Next, Europe?) in idem., *Mi és a világ*. Budapest: Magyar Szemle Alapítvány, 2015, 275–280; idem.: "Változatok az európai integráció jövőjére" (Variations on the Future of European Integration), in idem., *Nyitás és identitás*, Szeged: Pólay Elemér Alapítvány, 2018, 151–156.

derway years ago, mainly in the area of international trade and investment, mostly due to technological advance and security policy considerations, and the pandemic will hasten this slowdown and also further fragmentation, regionalization, and localization, which were also already underway. The qualitative leap in digitalization triggered by the pandemic however is giving new impetus to other dimensions of global relations. In geopolitical and security terms, the process of strategic rivalry and the consequent escalation of confrontation and mutual mistrust that began years ago, particularly between the United States and China, is not slowing down but fast-tracking. The pandemic and the crisis it has triggered can intensify not only individual but also collective neurosis, making the world less safe and more dangerous.

The world is therefore constantly changing at varying speeds and in varying directions, and it is the phenomenon of change that we perceive most acutely and devote most attention to. It is also human nature that we perceive and feel change as overwhelmingly negative, despite the fact that the world has actually changed to the better, not the worse, in terms of key indicators over the last two thousand and also the last seventy years.[3]

It also follows that the elements of continuity and permanence tend to receive less attention, while change attracts more attention, prompts reflection, the drawing of conclusions, the making of proposals for even larger-scale changes, or—perhaps engendering trouble—the advancement of all-encompassing theories and ideologies. The very essence of a conservative worldview is to seek and find elements of permanence, to preserve lasting values even in the face of changes to the contrary. While a progressive approach would want to accelerate changes "required by historical necessity," a conservative one would attempt to slow them down at least. Change per se is therefore not a good or positive phenomenon, even if it is inevitable. The only way to preserve values is to recognize and accept the elements of permanence.

The elements of permanence are borne not only by the world but by European integration as well, and not only in its fundamental values and impressive results but also in its contradictions, dilemmas, challenges, and recurrent, often cumulative, crises. Challenges and crises call for new approaches, changes, "reforms" (small wonder that "crisis" and "reform" are the two most

---

[3] Rosling, Hans, *Factfulness: Ten Reasons We're Wrong About the World - and Why Things Are Better Than You Think*. London: Sceptre, 2018, 341.

frequently used words in the history of integration), but values are constant, as are dilemmas, even if they recur in different concrete forms and trigger "crises." Fifteen years ago, in the context of the defeat of the Constitutional Treaty, I pointed out that the process of European integration gained decisive momentum, for example, following the crisis triggered by the French National Assembly's *sine die* adjourning of ratification of the Treaty establishing the European Defence Community on 30 August 1954.[4]

Debated from the very outset, one of the most frequently mentioned and most important dilemmas is the question whether the creation of European unity should be based on cooperation and alliances among independent sovereign states (nations) or on a "supranational" federal structure to be established gradually. The debate is usually reduced to the opposition between sovereignists and federalists, although the variations are much more nuanced, and even this contrast is more complex. It does not make the issue any easier that the concepts themselves have not been clarified, nor can they be as long as the debate is fought over in the political arena.

We Hungarians immediately collide with the concept of the nation because we start out from the cultural concept of the nation[5] and therefore do not identify the nation and the state. Sovereignty, on the other hand, is basically a category international law accords only to the state and has nothing to do with the cultural nation. From a linguistic point of view, the word *nation* is not a problem, but our Hungarian word for it, *nemzet,* does not mean the same thing. With a view to European integration, this was why I came to the idea of a "supra-state Europe of nations" in an essay written twenty-five years ago and published in 2015.[6] The essay's idea being that European integration must maintain and strengthen national identities, because without them there will be no diverse—and united—Europe, but that the all-powerful, homogenous nation-state must weaken and move towards a stronger federal structure in which the aim is not to weaken but to strengthen national communities.

The question is, of course—and this is the second conceptual debate—what exactly do we mean by federation and federalism. A quasi-state with a

---

4   Martonyi, János, *Mi és a világ*. Budapest: Magyar Szemle Alapítvány, 2015, 275.
5   See Sólyom, László, "A kulturális nemzet fogalmáról és elismertetéséről," in idem., *Documenta* volume 3, *Közélet*. Budapest: HVG-ORAC, 2019, 341.
6   Martonyi, János, *Európa, nemzet, jogállam*. Budapest: Magyar Szemle – Európai Utas, 2015, 126.

unitary structure, controlled and directed from above, a kind of empire, the essence of which is that the Member States give up their sovereignty and transfer it to a "federal" structure, as it were, to central power? Or do we mean a bottom-up association of free communities—above all the nation as a historically evolved cultural, linguistic, and spiritual community—which preserve and live out their community identity. It would be very helpful to return to the original theological and philosophical roots of federalism and of the freedom of communities, to return to Christian communities and to Johannes Althusius, regarded as the father of federalism.[7] And it was from these roots that the federalist dream of European integration should have sprung. Unfortunately, this was not the case, and today a large part of European public opinion distrusts the concept itself, because it identifies it with the imperial practice of top-down superstate "federalism," of which, unfortunately, the reality of integration, combined with ideological motives, has provided and continues to provide ample examples.

The recognition of a historically established, primary linguistic, cultural, and spiritual community identity, i.e., national identity, and the political and institutional consequences that follow from this, has been a prerequisite for successful European integration from the outset. This is particularly true today, in a context of accelerating changes in the global economic and geopolitical world order, the demographic, political, and economic loss of ground by European and Western civilization in general, and of the recurrent and cumulative crises of the European integration process. And these processes are likely to intensify rather than weaken in the future, and the challenges and crises that they lead to no wisdom can foretell.

The other fundamental condition is the correct interpretation of federalism, also based on historical and history-of-ideas antecedents, the recognition and effective realization of the existence and cohesion of free, bottom-up communities and, arising from this, their cultural, economic, and political rights, in a word, their autonomy. Free communities, able to assume and assert their identity, can enter into alliances, associate in various political and institutional forms or unite in broader communities, and develop, alongside their

---

7   Hueglin, Thomas, "Federalism at the Crossroads: Old Meanings, New Significance." *Canadian Journal of Political Science*, volume 36 (2003), number 2, 275–294. https://doi.org/10.1017/S0008423903778639.

basic, primary national identity, a broader community identity, a European identity, also with historical roots, an *"espace de civilisation,"* a *"communauté spirituelle et culturelle,"*[8] as Schuman envisioned it, and then build on this a solid economic and political integration.

The two conditions must therefore be met together, and European integration must be built on the free federation of cultural national communities. This does not mean the disappearance of sovereignty in the sense of constitutional and international law and of the sovereign state, which is territorially organized (i.e., it has borders) and a subject of international law. The basic functions of the state derive from sovereignty and are linked to a specific territory. In the event of an external attack or threat, it is primarily the state that must provide protection, but the situation is similar in the case of, for example, an epidemic. Borders are needed, because, although diseases know no borders, even medieval cities were protected by walls against potentially dangerous outsiders, and, a disaster striking, the city gate could be closed, with all its negative consequences. The sovereign state can never give up certain existential functions, because to do so would be to lose its essence and its raison d'être. (Unfortunately, there have been several instances of this in our history. This is why it is essential that we have never lost our national identity, our nation, which is more important than our state, and which we will never lose "whatever happens.") It is worth emphasizing again at this point that joining European integration, sovereign Member States do not relinquish their sovereignty in whole or in part but entrust the exercise of some of their rights to common EU institutions and thereby exercise those powers jointly.

A sovereign state that recognizes the identity and autonomy of its linguistic, cultural, and spiritual communities is just as strong and secure as the European integration institutional system based on national communities, which likewise respects the sovereignty and constitutional identity of its Member States.

The combination and linked implementation of the cultural concept of the nation and a genuine bottom-up federalism would thus provide the "community of communities," or, in other words, the "supra-state Europe of na-

---

8   Georges-Henri Soutou, *La déclaration Schuman*. Académie des sciences morales et politiques, May 5, 2020. https://academiesciencesmoralesetpolitiques.fr/2020/05/05/georges-henri-soutou-la-declaration-schuman/

tions," as dreamed of twenty-five years ago. This could resolve the contradiction between concepts of a "Europe of nations" and a "supranational Europe," and, ultimately, would lead to a reconciliation between sovereignists and federalists (which has little likelihood at present).

It is true, that the chances of achieving a "supra-state Europe of nations" and a "community of communities," based on the link between the cultural concept of nation and a bottom-up federal structure, are currently slim. In fact, the idea is supported by neither sovereignists nor federalists. Sovereignists obviously fear for the continuation of the state with unlimited sovereignty in theory and in law (though limited in fact). The idea seems particularly dangerous to those who identify state sovereignty with the homogeneous nation-state, since, for them, the existence of any linguistic, cultural, or national community that cannot be identified with the state, or the recognition of some form of autonomy embodying its cultural, economic, and political rights, is tantamount to an attempt to break up their unitary nation state. They do not realize that the inclusion of sub-state community identities and the community rights based on them, the recognition of some form of cultural or territorial autonomy in this context, would not weaken but strengthen the unity and sovereignty of their state. It is unfortunate that in some important countries, the demand for autonomy has been replaced by a desire for secession and the formation of an independent state, which in turn genuinely threatens the unity and even the very existence of the state in question, thus providing arguments for those who oppose autonomy. However, it must be seen that the historical, geographical, demographic, ethnic, and cultural circumstances in the various countries are different, and autonomy is an appropriate solution for the coexistence of different national communities in a single sovereign state in the vast majority of cases.

Yet representatives of "superstate" federalism likewise disagree with integration based on connecting the cultural concept of the nation and bottom-up federalism. Their aim is to extend competences to supranational level, either within the framework of the Treaties, or through the competence creep that EU institutions—especially but not exclusively the Commission and Parliament—have a predilection for exercising or through the amendment of the Treaties. What is at stake here, then, is essentially the division of competences between the Member States and the EU institutions, the definition of the levels of decision-making, which is undoubtedly the most important issue in the institutional system. That is why it must be approached with great caution. Flexibility and selectivity are needed, and, instead of general theories and political dogmas ("ever closer union"), different approaches are needed in different areas. While joint action should be strengthened in areas primarily related to the external manifestation of sovereignty (external and internal security, foreign policy, defence), a reasonable balance should be found between EU, national, and subnational levels of decision-making in others.

The situation though is not hopeless. Progress has been made in strengthening regionalism, and the concept of subsidiarity, initially treated as formulaic and taken less seriously, is beginning to take on more substance. Here, too, we should return to the Schumanian idea of spiritual and cultural community, based on Christianity and democracy.[9] For these are the two most important and complementary elements of subsidiarity: there is no subsidiarity without the interdependent system of Christian communities and their freedom and democratic functioning. Could this not be the federalism of democratic, free "communitie" that grounds and holds together the "espace de civilisation" borne of Christianity? In no way is this at odds with the establishment of Community and EU competences and their joint exercise through the EU institutions. Provided that it complies with the order and principles established by the Treaties and is based on the non-discriminatory application of the rule of law, in both the relationship between international legal norms and EU law and between EU law and Member States. This structure needs stronger involvement of the linguistic, cultural, and spiritual communities within and beyond the Member States, communities which mean the very heart of the European "espace de civilisation" and diversity.

A step in the right direction could be the recognition of national regions in different forms and legally, too.[10] The Commission's initial rejection of the recognition of these regions—which the Court of Justice subsequently had to correct—indicates the aversion of the "centre," not quite fittingly referred to as "Brussels," to historical, linguistic, spiritual, cultural, and "civilisational" factors, which not only denies the Schumanian legacy but is now one of the main obstacles to the successful continuation of the European integration process.

---

9 Ibid.
10 European Citizens' Initiative: Cohesion policy for equality between regions and the sustainability of regional cultures. European Commission, Brussels, 30 April 2019.

This brings us to the second main dilemma of European integration, the imbalance that characterizes the relationship between the economic and the political dimensions of integration, the dominant and successful dimension being, no doubt, economic integration, the common tariff and trade policy, the common and then single market, the successful competition policy, the almost too successful agricultural policy and the single currency, which, of course, in the absence of adequate preparation and economic and budgetary policy foundations, has raised and continues to raise serious dilemmas. Overall, however, economic integration is one of the greatest successes in the history of Europe.

The efforts to achieve political unity lag far behind the successes of economic integration, the most obvious sign of which is the very poor performance of the common foreign and security policy and common defence. This is so in spite of the fact that the whole enterprise, the original the Schumanian idea, was about political unity—the cause, the origin, the goal was essentially political (*"finalité politique"*)—, and economic integration was only a means to that end. It is true that it was an indispensable instrument, all the more so because political ends and economic means were inseparable when the Community of Coal and Steel was created. The technical, functional, and incremental nature of the Monnet method, which was created at the time and later extended, was well suited to the needs of the gradual development of economic integration, but it could not strengthen the political dimension.[11]

More important than the imbalance between the economic and the political dimension, however, is the third, and in fact the most important dimension, the relegation of the cultural sphere to the background, the eclipse of the Schumanian "espace de civilisation" and "communauté culturelle et spirituelle." This was to have been the motor, the heart and soul of the whole enterprise. Not for nothing did we talk so much about the soul of Europe, though we have done and are doing little. This soul, "l'âme de l'Europe," would presuppose first and foremost general recognition of a community identity. There can be no individual identity without a community identity, just as there can be no community or collective identity without the individually

---

11   Reho, Federico Ottavio, *Future of Europe: For a New Europeanism*. Brussels: Wilfried Martens Centre for European Studies, 2017. https://www.martenscentre.eu/wp-content/uploads/2020/06/future-europe-new-europeanism.pdf.

assumed and chosen identities of the individuals belonging to the community. It is this cultural-civilizational dimension, European identity, that—as I wrote in my 2017 essay on the Future of Europe—must be put in the centre of European integration.

The way to return to our original goals is to rediscover our roots, our essence, our nature, and our being unto ourselves. There is no problem with giving priority to different elements of this identity. We understand if someone notices Greek temples before the cathedral of Notre-Dame, and we accept the ancient heritage as an indispensable element of European identity, without which Europe would not be what it is. We respect and accept the Enlightenment and its values, freedom, equality, and fraternity, without which Europe would not be what it is. But neither would Europe be what it is without its Judeo-Christian heritage. The essence of Europe is "civilisation chrétienne," to return to Schuman. All these values together have made and shaped European identity, which cannot do without any of these elements of cultural and spiritual heritage. Alongside the Acropolis and Golgotha, the Capitoline also played an important role, for, without the legacy of Roman law, law could not have been an indispensable instrument in establishing and running the Community institutions, developing integration (legal norms and rulings have been particularly important instruments in the development of the economic dimension of integration), and a central element of culture itself, European identity.

European identity therefore has several—at least three—indispensable substantive elements, and together they constitute the diversity that is perhaps the greatest advantage of the European "espace de civilisation" over other cultures. Part of this has to do with the fact that the emphasis is not placed on the same element—or "Hill"—due to different historical and cultural reasons or even political and economic interests. However, it can be a serious problem when we fail to respect the most important values of others and to recognize that they are important not only for those who believe in them but also as an inescapable part of European culture as a whole and European identity. The problem can be exacerbated if we forget the Schumanian idea, the foundational principle of "civilisation chrétienne," when European integration comes to a juncture, perhaps a critical and fateful point in time.

Differences in approaches to the essence of European identity can become a serious challenge to integration when these differences create, maintain, and exacerbate divisions between the actors of integration, especially between the Member States, which are difficult to resolve. This brings us to the third major dilemma of integration: internal conflicts and the resulting divisions with varying substance and form.

Currently, the "West–East" divide is in the limelight, though the past seventy years have seen a number of other divisions, as is the case today too. Undoubtedly, the most important factor at the outset was the Franco–German reconciliation brought about by successive historical events and prominent statesmen, and without which European integration would not have happened. However, the interests of the two dominant countries clashed severally in the integration process—recall the six months of *la chaise vide*, the difficulties of British accession, or the disagreements over the introduction of the euro and enlargement to the east, which were resolved in time and then reappeared in other forms. Clearly, the relationship, understanding, and cooperation between these two countries, or their lack, continue to play a decisive role in the life of the European Union and in the process of integration. However, true historical recollection will not hide the fact that, in addition to the current cooperation between the two countries, the fate of integration is influenced by many other economic and political factors and interests linked to the relationship among the Member States.

The North–South divide, not touched upon here, has been shaped largely by economic interests, and the current debates are also largely influenced by these economic and financial interests and the related views on economic policy. The basic economic philosophical approaches and the resulting models have never been uniform, and the heated debate on the eurobond, for example, has much to do with these historically defined divergent models, views, and interests. However, their outcome will determine the future of integration, in not only the eurozone but the European Union as a whole.

The East–West divide is of a different nature. Here too, there are disputes over economic matters, specifically money, but the real debate is more complex and deeper, much more about cultural heritage, identity, lack of knowledge, sensitivity, mutual distrust and misunderstanding, political and moral superiority, inferiority and superiority complexes, and much more, which will not be easy to process and resolve.

Seventy years ago, things did not start off badly in spite of the far worse conditions. Let us go back to the words of Schuman, who made it clear that the peoples of Central and Eastern Europe, deprived of their freedom by a totalitarian regime, would join the European Community as soon as they were able to do so.[12] Speaking at Jagiellonian University in Kraków in September 1967 (Marxist-Leninist French students would not allow him to speak at the Sorbonne), the most eminent proponent of the concept of the Europe of Nations, President Charles de Gaulle, sent a subtle yet firm message that foreign occupation and totalitarianism would one day come to an end.[13]

Indeed, the *annus mirabilis* did come, East-Central Europe was transformed, and so were Europe and the world. German reunification took place. It may sound like something of a bon mot, but the hard reality was that Hungarian public opinion and politics were more united in favour of German reunification than was German public opinion… (not to mention France and the United Kingdom, of course). Hungarians and other Central Europeans not only felt that Germany's division was politically and morally untenable, they also knew that, without German reunification, there could be no reunification of Europe.

This was how German unity was created, and—after a decade and a half passed—Europe was united. The extent to which this unification becomes a reality, how it permeates all its economic, political, and cultural dimensions, whether it enters the souls of Western and Eastern Europeans, depends on all of us Western and Eastern Europeans.

From here at the eastern edge, subjectively and with traditional Central European sensibilities, it seems that perhaps less virtue signalling, less finger pointing, less playing the blame game, and, yes, less patronizing might be needed from the other side. Unravelling the details would require a separate study, which will probably require waiting until the current extraordinary situation and the resulting unrest pass.

The three dilemmas—the conflict between sovereignists and federalists, the imbalance among the economic, political, and cultural dimensions of integration, and the conflicts and divisions among Member States—and several other challenges have not only been with us throughout of the last seven decades but will in all likelihood remain with us in the future. The big ques-

---

12 *"Quant aux pays d'Europe centrale et orientale aujourd'hui privés de liberté par un régime totalitaire, ils rejoindront l'Europe communautaire, n'en doutons pas, dès qu'ils le pourront"* quoted by Soutou, 2020.
13 Peyrefitte, Alain, *C'était de Gaulle*. Paris: Gallimard, 2002, 60–61.

tion is how the current exceptional situation, the psychological, economic, and social shock of the pandemic, will affect, accelerate or slow down and alter the direction of the processes of change in the world in general. And, in this context, how will it impact the present and future of European integration. Will pessimistic prognosticators be right in pointing out a series of developments detrimental to integration, or will it turn out once again that the process of European unity is deeper and stronger than it appears on the surface, and that the crisis, as ever before, did not curb but has, on the contrary, strengthened and furthered it. The answer will depend crucially on getting to the heart of the matter, on rediscovering the key elements of community and European identities, on recognizing that the foundations of civilization and culture are more important than anything else, since they determine, among other things, the key factors of global competition, demography and technological development. The most important question is whether we can draw from the crisis a new energy, momentum, and determination to renew the integration process in a real and meaningful way.

Some things change, some remain unchanged. This was how Novalis grieved, not 70 years ago but 221: "Those were beautiful, magnificent times, when Europe was a Christian land, when one Christianity dwelled on this civilized continent, and when one common interest joined the most distant provinces of this vast spiritual empire."[14]

---

14 Novalis, Friedrich, "Christianity or Europe: A Fragment" (1799), in *The Early Political Writings of the German Romantics*, ed. Frederick C. Beiser. Cambridge: Cambridge University Press, 1996, 61.

European Identity – To Open up or Close in

Delivered at the University of Public Service, Budapest, 6 October 2020

In the 1950s, efforts to create a European political community intensified. The proposals for the establishment of a European Defence Community and a European Political Community were put forth, but, to the surprise of many at the time, they were voted down by the French National Assembly. This prompted the idea, particularly to Robert Schuman, Jean Monnet and others, that economic integration should be put on the agenda in this situation. Its precursor, the European Coal and Steel Community, had already been founded, providing a model for how economic integration—at least in a specific sector—could be achieved. Its institutional framework had been put in place by the Paris Treaty establishing the European Coal and Steel Community, the essence of which remains unchanged to this day. Economic integration was therefore launched, and the process of creating political union would be added to it later. Major institutional changes were made in due course, which gradually extended, modified, shaped, and deepened the whole institutional make-up: Maastricht, Amsterdam, Nice, and, following the Constitutional Treaty, the Lisbon Treaty, which did not create a new, separate treaty, but amended the Treaty of Rome.

Unlike to the main features of economic integration and institutional development, less attention has been paid to the basis of this whole process. What was it based on, and why was the integration process launched? Why do many people think that what we have achieved must be preserved? Why do so many of us think that it must be constantly reformed and improved? In some respects, we need to go further along the path of integration. In some things we need to show more moderation, or even to take a step back. We therefore continue to think about how to take this process forward on the basis of a multi-faceted, selective approach. But we may not always understand the essence of the process. The essence of European integration is not necessarily to be found in the material sphere—not in politics, not in economics, not even in geopolitics, important as it is—but rather it is deeper than that: in our minds, in culture in the broadest sense of the word. It is thus the essence of Europe we must seek and find, and we must ask ourselves whether there is a European identity, and, if there is a European identity, what its essence is.

These are the most important questions concerning the European integration process. They are more important than economic integration, the importance of which we do not underestimate, not least because it is by far the most successful dimension of European integration. But not everything in the world is determined by the economy. There has been an ideology that says that everything is rooted in the economy, that everything is determined by the economy. It has been wrong. It is not at all clear whether religious wars are rooted in economic, political or even power factors. There are other, more important factors that determine the lives of individuals and communities, and history in general. It is this intellectual and cultural dimension that we need to approach and understand in the case of European integration too.

Identity is a subject matter that is addressed by a wide range of disciplines. Originally anthropological, its concept has also attracted the interest of psychology and later sociology. It is also relevant in law. In private international law, for example, an important question is how to define one's personal law. What is considered to be governing for the individual person? Do we consider the law of the country of which he is a citizen or the law of the country in which he is settled to be his personal law? Some legal systems bind personal law to citizenship, others—the law of the Anglo-American countries—to domicile, residence taken up with a permanent settlement intention. For some, territory is the more important determining factor, and for others it is citizenship. The basis of citizenship also matters: what is the most important relationship between a person and the state? For some people, this relationship is essentially the place of residence, the territory of the state where one lives, and for others, citizenship is determined by the country of which one's ancestors, parents, grandparents, etc., were citizens. If that is the case, the question arises as to whether, if someone's parents or grandparents were Hungarian citizens, the only decisive factor should be whether their ancestors lived in Subotica or Szeged, Oradea or Debrecen, or in Košice or Miskolc. This has led to the recognition of Hungarian citizenship for cross-border Hungarians, and to the possibility for them to acquire Hungarian citizenship on the basis of their ancestors. These are also issues related to identity.

Identity became really interesting when it entered politics. Identity also raises problems in the individual sphere, and the identity of the individual is also a thrilling issue. Individuals tend to have multiple identities; indeed, few have a single one, belong to a single community. We are Hungarians, we belong to the Hungarian nation as a community. At the same time, of course, we can also be members of a religious community, which can play a very important role in our lives. We can be Hindus, Buddhists, Muslims, Jews, Christians, Catholics or Protestants, all of these are important communities. We can belong to a political party, a political movement. Identity can also be important, and unfortunately it has sometimes played a far too important role in people's lives. What can be very dangerous is exclusive identity. There are quite a few examples of this in history. In a novel by Lyudmila Ulitskaya, a Soviet youth so exclusively identifies with the Bolshevik Party, his Bolshevik identity, that he reports his father to the NKVD.

If one can have multiple identities, it follows that identities can clash. Greek tragedies memorably present it, and there have been many examples up to our day. The martyrs of Arad decided that they were not Austrian officers but Hungarian patriots, defected to the Hungarian army, and paid for it with their lives. A further example points to an even sharper conflict between identities. A Hungarian politician participated in the communist movement from an early age, became a convinced communist, and lived in the Soviet Union, with all the consequences that entailed. Then, in 1956, he became prime minister on popular demand, but he was still a member of the Communist Party. At one point, he had to decide which of his identities—Hungarian or Communist—came first. He decided twice: first, on 28 October 1956, when he gave the order to stop the fighting and then to integrate the revolutionaries and the National Guard into the regular army and to set up a new revolutionary coalition government. His first decision was thus to side with the freedom fighters. It could be said was compelled by circumstances. But he also had another decision to make. In custody in Romania, he was visited and invited to return home, sign some papers. He would not be harmed and might even get a decent little job. He thought it through, and, knowing he would be executed, he refused to sign the paper. His original communist identity clashed with his national identity, his Hungarianness. This man, Imre Nagy, decided that his Hungarian identity, his belonging to the Hungarian nation, was more important. And he became a martyr.

Individual identity can change. You are free to choose your identity, meaning you can change it in your lifetime. We know from the poet: "Let him who swaps his homeland swap his heart." It is not so easy to change one's homeland or nationality, but examples abound.

What makes this topic really interesting at the moment is not so much individual, personal identity but community identity. With community identity, the first question is whether there is one at all. According to many, each individual has a belonging, a self-identity, but communities cannot be endowed with such a quality as an identity. This is where the political debate starts out from, which is on-going throughout the world. There are those who see community identity as dangerous and call identity politics tribal, nativist or worse. They always refer to the excesses of communal identity because there are examples of it in history, and this is the basis of the mistrust of and political aversion to communal identity.

However, community identity does exist, and therefore a community has its own identity, its own essence, which is made up of the identity of the individuals belonging to the community. Individuals derive their identity from the community, and the community derives its identity from individuals. The concept and meaning of nation presuppose the identity of the nation as a community, which cannot be limited to territory alone. It is not certain that national identity, the sense of belonging to a nation, is tantamount to living in the territory of a nation. In the case of Hungary, the borders of nation and state, and consequently the concepts of nation and state, do not coincide. We therefore need a separate concept of nation. The cultural concept of nation dates back to the nineteenth century French religious historian and philosopher Ernest Renan—as it happens, a favourite author of President de Gaulle.

A nation is thus a mental, intellectual, linguistic, and cultural community rooted in history, which is undoubtedly influenced by territorial factors and state borders, but a national community is not necessarily bound to a territory and cannot be identified with belonging to a state. If we recognize the identity of this cultural community, then a nation, a national community, must also have rights. This brings us to the category of community rights, that is to say, collective rights in terms of both constitutional and international law, which is a subject of continuing debate to our day. We have not been able to have the collective rights of national minorities be accepted by international conventions; only the individual rights of persons belonging to national minorities are recognized, even in European legal instruments.

Why is community identity important? First of all, because it is the way to build the most important community identity—national identity. This identity is not exclusive, but it is the primary identity for most Europeans. In Europe, the primary, the most important community identity is national identity. If we want to strengthen European identity, it is essential not only to recognize community identity but also to accept, recognize, and strengthen national identity based on linguistic, cultural, and spiritual communities. This will lead to a diverse but existing European identity.

If we cannot accept the existence of community identity, including national identity, we will not be able to understand European identity. The two are therefore linked: we must first accept national identity as the defining primary affiliation, and this can lead us to European identity, its recognition and underpinning.

If we agree that there is European identity, the next question is what the substance of that identity is. The starting point is diversity, a word included in Article 3(3) of the Treaty of Lisbon. What can be debated is what the most important elements of this European identity are. In 1976, Helmut Kohl said that Europe is, first, a *Geschichtsraum,* a historical space; second, a *Kulturraum,* a cultural space, and third, a *Wertegemeinschaft,* a community of values. And Robert Schuman had said seventy years ago that Europe is an *espace de civilisation.* He did not say that Europe stretches from the Atlantic to Vienna, as Metternich had said, or to the Urals, as de Gaulle would later do, but that Europe is a space of civilization, a cultural space, and therefore its essence is cultural identity.

European identity has been and still is much discussed. If we want to understand European identity, it is of course useful to read works on the philosophy of history, but the easiest way is to go out into the streets and see what surrounds us. What do we see? First of all, we see a lot of crosses, not only on churches but also in cemeteries, public spaces, on the roads, and in all kinds of artworks. The first thing someone coming from another planet would ask is what all these crosses mean here, what their message is. Then at noon we hear the bells ringing, and we even hear peals on holidays and at funerals. We see crosses, and we hear bells, all this points to something in common, some belonging together.

What else do we see in Europe? In galleries and public spaces, we see sculptures and paintings of people, often naked human bodies. Some civilizations prohibit the depiction of people, and even more so the depiction of the naked human body. And we have been depicting the human body for thousands of years. We are proud of the beauty of the human body, that is why we represent it. In other civilizations it is strictly forbidden. This is rooted in ancient culture. We tend to identify our ancient roots and heritage as the second most important source of European identity after Christianity. Europe would not exist without the Greco-Roman heritage, learning, and arts, and we are therefore particularly grateful to the Renaissance, because this rebirth brought the ancient heritage, with all its beauty and knowledge, back into our culture, into our identity. Not so long ago, President Macron made an eloquent speech about Europe, in which he said that there is indeed a European identity. He said that wherever you go, you see Greek temples. There are indeed Greek temples in Europe, but President Marcon did not say, although he made this famous speech at the Sorbonne, that a few hundred metres away there is the cathedral of Notre Dame, which you can perhaps see from the Sorbonne. One of the cornerstones of European identity is precisely Notre Dame and the presence of cathedrals all over Europe. The focus is thus not always the same, but ultimately, if we can agree that there is a Judaeo-Christian tradition, which is a cardinal element of this *espace de civilisation*, then we can also agree that, yes, there is an antique heritage. We can also agree that there are a number of other aspects of European history that are incorporated into European identity. The ideas of freedom, equality, and fraternity were also built into it in the wake of the Enlightenment.

Moreover, there is something else that we see in all Europe. We have noted the cross, the ancient statues and paintings, but, in the main square of almost every European city we see a large and imposing building. It is the building of the court, the court of justice, prominent everywhere. It is the building where justice is administered, even though justice has not always been done in these buildings. There would be no European civilization, no European cultural space without law, and that is why we say that the third most important root and factor of Europe is law, and the basis of this is the Roman legal heritage. This brings us to the Three Hills: the Acropolis as a symbol of ancient culture, Golgotha as a symbol of the Judeo-Christian tradition, and the Capitoline as a symbol of Roman law. The legal systems of all European countries ultimately grew out of Roman law. The vast majority of European countries' legal systems have adopted, adapted, and interiorized Roman law, including German, French, Swiss, and Hungarian law. There is one legal system—the English one—that has not done so, yet it is English legalese that uses Latin terms the most.

In European history, there are antecedents not only of sovereign statehood but also of political unity. The establishment of sovereign states with territorially defined borders is usually associated with the Treaty of Westphalia in 1648. That peace fixed borders, set down that we accepted the fact that there were people of other religions beyond the borders, and also established a kind of balance—what we now call geopolitics—which would keep us from starting another thirty-year religious war. But Europe also had a Roman Empire, then a Frankish Empire, and then a Holy Roman Empire, which was not a real political unity but gave Europe a framework. And there too was the *Respublica* of the peoples, the nations of Europe, the *Respublica Christiana*, the Christian Commonwealth, and so we are back to Christianity, the essence of European identity. If we accept that Europe has an identity, and that these three elements are present in it, then we can even argue about their order, but let us not argue about one thing: diversity and the tolerance it implies.

If we accept that there is a European identity, is there a Central European identity? For we talked a lot about Central Europeanness in historical, economic, and political terms, especially during and after the period of regime-change. It was not by chance that we established the Central European Free Trade Association, and that we launched the Visegrád Cooperation. The idea of Central Europe therefore appeared as soon as it had an opportunity to do so in recent history. Our Central European cooperation efforts turned our belonging culturally together, our heritage, a cultural dimension, into an economic and political reality. What cinema, literature, poetry our culture in general had long expressed, we were able to transform into an economic and political actuality as soon as history, the Soviet Union withdrawing from the region, occasioned it.

What then is the essence of Central European identity? Central European identity is in fact the same as the European identity, but denser, more fast paced, perhaps more intent, and filled with more tensions. Central Europe has many languages and several religions in a relatively small area and has even greater diversity due to the mosques in its southern regions. It has at least two types of cross, owing to the presence of Orthodoxy. It had the greatest number synagogues until the Holocaust. This is a more condensed and impassioned, a hastier Europe than Europe in general. We are said to be melancholic, even pessimistic, and also funnier—our special sense of humour having been shaped by a rougher history. We are said to be creative; we Hungarians in particular tend to pride ourselves on our Nobel Prize winners and creativity. We are also said to be a bit neurotic, prone to complexes, an inferiority complex for instance, all also obviously shaped by history. Some say we have a superiority complex, precisely because of the sense of inferiority. All this is debatable, but it is certain that there is a specific Central Europeanness.

As far as religious tolerance is concerned, it was the Hungarian National Assembly sitting at Torda [today Turda, in Romania] that first proclaimed religious freedom and religious tolerance in Europe in 1568—it was indeed unprecedented on the continent at the time. Central Europeanness is with us and is coming to the fore more and more. As regards national and European identity, two points need to be kept in mind. One is that national identity in Central European countries is more strongly linked to Christianity than in Western Europe. During the debate in the European Convention drawing up the draft Treaty establishing a Constitution for Europe on whether to refer to Europe's Christian roots in the text, the majority of Central Europeans supported the reference. Largely as a result of French opposition, it was not included in the draft, and thus never made it into the Treaty of Lisbon.

Throughout its history, Central Europe has often suffered external attack. These threatened both our Christianity and our national identity, in other words, our very national existence. We Hungarians are wont to say that our history is that of survival—the British historian Bryan Cartledge has published a book entitled *The Will to Survive: A History of Hungary*. We had to survive external attacks threatening both our Christianity and our very national existence. Western European nations have fought serious wars against each other: the English and the French the Hundred Years' War, Germans and Germans the Thirty Years' War. None of these wars posed existential threats to the respective nations and their identity. The stakes in these wars were whether England or France would be the stronger power, whether Germany would be Protestant or Catholic, but for us the fight was not about that but about whether or not we would survive as a nation and as Christians. Consequently, both Christianity and Europe were more important for us. Had the Ottomans occupied the whole country and turned it into a Turkish province for good, our survival as a nation would hardly have been assured. Thus, our national identity was inextricably linked to Christianity and Europe. That is why both Christianity and belonging to Europe are important to us here in Central Europe.

The Constitutional Treaty was rejected by the majority of the voters in the referenda in two of the founding Member States, France and the Netherlands. All in all, it can be safely said that in Central Europe—especially in Poland and Hungary, the two countries most exposed to external attack—the sense of belonging to both Christianity and Europe is significantly stronger than either is in Western European countries.

The third element of European identity is embodied in the court building mentioned above: law. There had been important laws before Roman law, but Roman law was the first coherent system without which legal norms would not play the role they do today in every country in Europe.

By the accounts of history, everything in Europe came from somewhere. Without Egyptian civilization, there would have been no Crete; without Crete, there would have been no Greek culture, no antique learning, and no Rome. The monotheistic world religions have several elements in common, and humanity and civilizations conversed with each other in spite of the great distances between them. Hinduism had a major influence on Judaism and, through it, on Christianity. Islam was not a singular desert initiative but took over elements from numerous religions. Europe has a distinctive, well-definable identity. However, it has always been the most open continent in the world, absorbing external influences and thus having its hills: the Acropolis, the Capitoline, and Golgotha, and then after that starting to radiate its influence. Without the expansion of European civilization, the world would not be what it is today. Europe has given much to the world, however fashionable it is to question the achievements of this civilization. As a minor example, English law set foot in two thirds of the world, and those countries continue to base their institutions on English law. The imprint of European culture on the world is undeniable.

Europe has received much from the world and has given it much by eradiation. This eradiation can and must be continued, but it requires mending ourselves. We must be aware of ourselves, of what we are unto ourselves, our own essence. This would be European identity. There are other words to express this; Schuman, for example, called it *l'âme de l'Europe*, because Europe has a soul, it only needs to be able to find it. Our further integration hinges on this.

The seventy-year history of European integration has been a stunning success in the economy, a half success in politics, but the cultural dimension and thus the question of identity have in fact been neglected, notwithstanding the explicit mention of culture in the Founding Treaty. The single market and, after some jerks and dips, the single currency have come into being. Today, economic integration is making qualitative progress, provided that the NextGenerationEU funding is adopted and that powerful fiscal instruments are deployed alongside monetary policy instruments. We can even make progress in political and defence cooperation, but the fundamental question remains whether we can give the cultural dimension, identity, a more robust substance and expression. This could be the foundation of a spiritual community, a sense of belonging together, a demos on which real and strong political cooperation can be built. But this is a long process and should in no way be forced, for there are attempts to do so. A few days ago, the European Parliament's Committee on Constitutional Affairs heard two ideas for institutional reform: the *Spitzenkandidat* principle and the transnational list. I agree with neither, but that is not the point. The point is that we should try not to always look for institutional solutions. If we are going to have another big conference, so be it, but do not let us always think up institutional tricks to impose on people in order to get ahead.

Institutions and laws are very important, without them nothing would work. But we must realize that institutional solutions have their limits, and there are situations where we need to focus not on institutional and legal issues, not on new institutional reforms, but on how we can give substance to the process. More substance, stronger identity, better cohesion. The contribution of Central Europe can be greater than its economic and political significance, although things are not bad in this regard either. We have much to learn from each other, and diversity will only prevail if we are mutually ready to learn from one another.

I referred to the Peace of Westphalia above. Because both sides were Christian, one was Calvinist or Lutheran and the other Catholic, that treaty declared that we accept that some people practise their Christian faith differently. You have to accept and respect each other and not believe that one is inferior or superior to the other.

Demography is a key factor in global or universal history. Two important factors shape history in the long term, one is demography and the other is technology. Both demography and technology ultimately depend on people's minds. Europe is falling behind demographically, and we are unlikely to be able to reverse this demographic shrinkage. It needs to be counterbalanced in some way. One counterweight is a common foreign and defence policy and the strengthening of defence capabilities. Even in the ancient world, a demographically weakened city-state could compensate by strengthening its defence capabilities. Of course, this requires technology and political will. The whole process originally started with an overwhelmed, almost hopeless Europe and two superpowers, the United States and the Soviet Union. The Soviet Union was very close and getting closer. The United States helped Europe, making a major contribution to Europe's recovery and rise. Difficulties abounding, European integration nevertheless commenced. Thus, one way is to strengthen foreign policy and defence. The other counterweight is to strengthen identity.

The threat of Chinese identity or Chinese culture is often raised. The question is, of course, what Chinese identity is in fact. Is it Confucius? Buddha? Marx? Engels? Stalin? Mao Zedong? Or simply the cult of material prosperity and production? Wealth? If you asked the Chinese what they want to achieve in life, there is a presumption that ninety-nine out of a hundred would say they want to be rich. So Chinese identity is difficult to define, apart from the fact that there is a drive for power, economic and geopolitical expansion. The answer to the question whether China is a threat to European identity, whether there is an ideological threat, a threat to culture, to identity, is no. Instead, the issue that arises here is immigration, and that in the context of Islam. Some consider Islam to be a mortal danger, while others say that Islam has little power to conquer intellectually—that is, in terms of identity. Islam is in deep crisis. It finds it difficult to decide whether it is a political ideology—a means of gaining power like all ideologies—or a way of life or a religion. The religious element, transcendence, is weakening, political Islam is growing strong. Knives and bombs are not a way to successfully spread religion. It may have been possible in the past, in other civilizations, but it will not work in Europe. Violence is a sign of weakness. This is not to say, of course, that aggression should not be met with the firmest and toughest possible response. And that means prioritizing security alongside a stronger common foreign and defence policy. Security also includes the protection of borders. There is no state without borders, there is no Europe without borders. Borders must be protected. Throughout history, there have been great migrations, and they have been on-going for thousands of years. Events in 2015 were just a salutary warning shot that we should be careful, because there could be very big problems ahead. There have been two ways of removing people from their territory. One is war, the other is slow infiltration. We Hungarians could talk a lot about the latter. Borders must therefore be protected at all costs.

If we Europeans have our own identity and our own beliefs, then European culture cannot be weaker than Islam. I repeat, Islamist violence and terror are a sign of weakness. Many Islamic theologians see the problem in the fact that they let their religion lose the element of transcendence, which is the essence of all religions. Religion must be about faith, not power, not armed conquest, but something else, and if it is not about that, then it is stripped of meaning, and what remains is something that can only be spread by force. The use of terror is, in no small measure, about the struggle within Islam about which of the different tendencies will prove the strongest, whether extremist political Islam can gain the dominant role and lead a war against other civilizations.

Islam is not a part of the European cultural heritage, identity, even though Islam has been present in European history for a long time. European identity is different. Our understanding of the relationship between men and women is the primary difference. Polygamy in itself means that women can only be inferior; for if a man can have more than one wife, and the reverse is excluded, it is quite clear that equality of the two sexes is blocked. This is unacceptable to us. There are things that we cannot and must not accept, and that our legal system can never recognize. There is no polygamy in Europe, and there will never be any.

The fact that Europe is shrinking demographically and losing ground economically in the global system does not mean that we have to give up our identity and blend into something else. On the contrary! This is the main reason why we need to bolster the European integration process with a stronger identity, deploying moderation, clear-headedness, prudence, political strategy, and tact. We Belgians, Dutch, Czechs, Danes, and Hungarians will not be able to cope with this demographic and technological weakness on our own. The external threats and attacks from the global system are now not only threatening Central Europe. We are losing and will continue to lose serious ground in the global system if we do not reinforce our own edifice, our own system, and above all its cultural and intellectual energies and reserves.

European culture continues to play a bigger role in the world today than its place in global GDP would suggest. Europe still has significant advantages in both material and intellectual, cultural terms. It is still the largest and most important player in world trade. The European Union is the world's largest importer and exporter. It is not going to give up on this. In terms of eradiation, the European mind, not least European legal culture, continues to contribute at multilateral and universal levels. We have experience, we know how to reconcile the arrangements and legal norms of different conceptual frameworks. We therefore have experience in integration that no others have. Competition is under way, and the outcome cannot be predicted. We do know what it is reasonable to do if we want to have a chance.

We need to bolster people's European identity, but we should always be thoughtful in choosing the means to do so. I think European citizenship is one such means, because it can reinforce the sense of belonging to Europe. Freedom of movement is a fundamental factor, and a lot has happened in this area that would have been unthinkable fifty or sixty years ago. We have the single currency, and services, people, capital, and goods move freely, which is unprecedented. We should be thinking not in terms of institutional tricks but real results. There are many ideas, and the biggest problem with them is that they want institutional solutions and are after more and more institutional reforms. A significant number of people are fed up with these. This is not the area to look for solutions.

As for the external threats, I repeat: Islam is a serious issue, but let us not believe that it is a stronger religion, worldview, and outlook than ours. No, ours is stronger, but it has to be asserted by resolute means. Countries with large Islamic communities must ensure full transparency. We cannot allow separatism based on religious communities; we cannot have parallel societies. There have always been and there will always be external influences, because without them, there would be no Europe. But Europe as a community also has an interest in ensuring that our descendants and their descendants preserve and pass on our values, our *Geschichtsraum*, our *Kulturraum*, our *Wertegemeinschaft*, and our *espace de civilisation*, which is the essence of our identity.